Faith Says What God Says

Intensive Prayer and Word Medication for
Renewing the Spirit of the Mind

By Harriett Ford

Copyright ©
H.L Ford 2019

All rights reserved.
Without limiting the rights under copyright
no part of this publication may be reproduced,
stored in a retrieval system or transmitted
in any form or by any means
(electronic, mechanical, photocopying,
recording or otherwise), without the prior written
permission of the copyright owner of this book.

ISBN: 9781793369550

Third Edition
Designed and Formatted by
Meredith House Publishing

Endorsements

Comments from pastors, ministries, best-selling inspirational authors, teachers, and people of faith:

Pastor Dan Zirkle of Our Finest Hour Church in Broken Arrow, OK and radio host of the highly respected *Our Finest Hour* broadcast on OASIS Radio Network:
"I have read Harriett Ford's booklet excerpted from *Faith Says What God Says*. She offers brief meditations and prayers and presents vital healing truths, examples of divine healing, and practical ideas for making the truth become reality for the doer of the Word. If you are looking for nuggets to build your faith, especially in the area of divine healing, this book will encourage your walk with the God of supernatural healing."

Dr. Marla Woodmansee, president and radio host of the highly popular *Kingdom Xperience* broadcast (FM 88.1, Branson, MO) and producer of the ***Kingdom Xperience* Magazine**, is a Bible communicator, women's conference speaker, and much more. She holds a Master's Degree from Assembly of God Theological Seminary and has studied abroad in Israel's Jerusalem University. She has been instrumental in bringing nationally known speakers to the 2019, "It Is Possible" Branson *Kingdom Xperience* 2019 Summit. See her web site at (www.marlawoodmansee.org):

"Harriett gives understanding and the full mind of God in this excellent book on healing. She encourages us to believe God's word and have faith to receive healing. Informative and empowering! I urged her to publish this collection of healing truths."

Doctor Dave Walker, practicing physician and author of the best-selling *God in the ICU*, (listed on Page One of Amazon for inspirational biographies) and *Prayer, Medicine and Miracles, Faith Adventures of a praying doctor:*

"This is not the sort of book one can just glance at. There is so much good content and so much wisdom, obviously gained from experience. I'm thoroughly enjoying it and applying much. One really needs it beside one's bed or in the closet of one's quiet time. It's also making me think. As you say early on, there are still mysteries in healing, but that should not stop us from continuing to do what Jesus did and pray for the sick."

Pastor Evelyn Gipson, of Rockford, Illinois has spent a lifetime of study and ministering on the subject of healing. Her book, *The Great Physician: Still on Call*, gives the reader an understanding of how to receive supernatural healing, how to walk in supernatural healing, and how to maintain and protect healing:

"I love what Harriet Ford does to encourage people to believe for healing. The testimonies are wonderful. I am blessed to know her. Having lots of miracles here. God is so good. Be blessed."

Faith Says What God Says

Intensive Prayer and Word Medication for
Renewing the Spirit of the Mind
to Receive Healing from the Word

"The Lord has given me a well-instructed tongue, that I may know how to sustain the weary one with a word. He wakens me in the morning to listen like one being instructed."
Isaiah, 50:4.

About the author...

Harriett Ford is a women's conference speaker, award-winning faith writer, board member of Dr. Marla Woodmansee's Kingdom Xperience program on KLFC Radio in Branson, MO., and a frequent contributor to the *American Christian Voice Magazine*. She has appeared as a guest speaker on *The Prophet Speaks* at *Morningside* TV show filmed near Branson, the Kevin Shorey Ministries TV program, and the Kingdom Xperience broadcast on KLFC radio. She can often be found at the Copper Coin, a Christian gifts and jewelry shop in Grand Village Mall in Branson, Mo. where she tells the story of Susan Abar-Berger's miraculous healing from incurable pancreatic cancer.

Contact her at **harrietf@centurytel.net** or visit her author's website at **HLfordbelieves.com** and **www.facebook.com/Harriettbarnettford**.

Her books include: *Shadow in the Rain, the Beyond Fantasy series, God Wants Me Well,* and *Supervention,* available at **www.amazon.com/Harriett-Ford**

For speaking engagements, email Harriett at:

harrietf@centurytel.net

"The Lord God performed great signs and mighty wonders in the land of Egypt and Israel, and <u>even to this day among the nations</u>."
Jeremiah 32: 21

INTRODUCTION

Don't believe in miracles? You will when you need one. The Lord shows me a huge veil over the minds of the traditional church when it comes to this subject, which makes it a controversial subject in many denominations. However, healing is the calling card of Jesus to say God has redeemed His people from the curse of the law by way of the cross. Healing is confirmation of His Divinity as the Son of God, according to **Luke 7:21**.

Why should anyone want to read anything written by me? I am a very ordinary, imperfect person with lots of flaws, mistakes, and weaknesses. However, I know the One who has none of these.

I know what He has downloaded into the realm of my listening and seeking heart. I know that He wants me to share it with others, who have lots of flaws, mistakes and weaknesses, so they can find He is Way, He is the One Who has set us free, not to live any which way our flesh desires, but to live free from the power of sin, and to lift us up out of the ordinary and into the realm of the impossible. He has done that for me. He will do it for you.

These daily healing words will help you do for yourself what no one else can do for you. Attend to God's word, continue in it, and learn how to receive by faith what God has promised. I will begin by saying that I do not know all the answers to the mystery of prayer for healing. God has mysteries. God has secrets **(Deut. 29: 29)**.

As always, the Number One question when it comes to praying for the sick is this: Why isn't everyone healed? Everyone at times will lose a loved one or a church member, while praying with all the faith he has, myself included. No one should ever feel guilty because of this. Even Jesus was not always successful at praying for the sick. In His own hometown of Nazareth, "He could do no mighty works there because of their unbelief," (**Matt. 13:58** and **Mark 6:5**). However, He did NOT stop praying for the sick. He never paused to ask, Father is it Your will to restore this person? Is this person good enough? His entire ministry clearly shows that healing is the Father's will.

We can't go wrong by following His example. Either Christ is our healer the same today, yesterday, and forever, or He is not Who He says He is. Why then does it seem that many times we have so little victory in dealing with sickness? Such a book as this will always provoke critics who want to argue the case for staying sick. I won't rob them of that opportunity. I will simply say there is life in the Word, and God is a rewarder of them who diligently seek Him.

Yes, it's true, devout believers and diligent seekers die every day. However, they do not have to die of illness. I do not doubt that God wants His people well. I have spent years of my life in the scriptures seeking answers to the many questions about God's supernatural healing. I have listened to thousands of sermons and teachings, read hundreds of books on the subject, interviewed numbers of people who have experienced supernatural healing. (See the Afterword at the end of the book.) I do not claim to have all the answers, but I have discovered some keys. The Lord has laid it on my heart to share them.

As you continue to meditate on and pray these scriptures, let the truth in them develop faith which comes through hearing and continuing in the Word. Faith is the evidence of things not seen. Renewing the mind to what God says is learning to walk by faith and not by sight, to believe what you do not yet see, until it manifests. Do not be discouraged if healing doesn't happen overnight. Cast not away your confidence.

You are not appointed to defeat. God wants His people to be victorious over-comers. Seek and you shall find.

†

Faith Says What God Says

Who would argue with that? Why, the devil, of course.

Most of us have read a promise in the Bible and immediately thought, I can't move a sycamore tree, much less a mountain simply by speaking to it. Who told you that? That's the fowls of the air stealing the Word (seed). That's doubt saying what the devil says.

When I began to understand the parable of the sower (Matt. 13; Luke 8 and Mark 4), I realized that at times I have allowed the cares of this world to choke out the word, and then given up on my harvest because I did not know how the seed works.

I determined to seek the Lord diligently. I wanted to plant the faith-seed in good soil so it puts down deep roots. I have to pull the weeds of doubt and wait patiently for the harvest—which is the promise I'm waiting on to manifest.

It doesn't usually happen overnight. The crows have to be chased away. Sunlight, nourishment and rain are needed. In Mark 11: 23, a believer keeps saying what God says, regardless of how impossible the challenge looks. Three times the word "say" is repeated in that parable. That's three times the saying what God says, instead of speaking doubt.

Please note, I am not speaking about sowing seed

for only personal wants and desires. The name-it-claim-it and confession-is-possession group certainly strayed into extremes. That's not what this book of meditations and example prayers is about.

Faith says what God says. If you don't have a prayer journal, get one. You will be writing several key verses as you go through this book. Write Isaiah 43: 26 in the prayer journal and begin to practice putting God in remembrance of His words in your daily prayers.

†

Who Told You That?

"Who told you that you were naked?" God asked Adam.

You know the story. The serpent beguiled Eve into thinking that with enough knowledge she could become like God. He lied to her by getting her to question God's word.

That's the same tactic Satan uses on everyone. Question God's Word: "*Has God said* you would die if you disobey?" Next, he tempts her with the lust of the eyes, the lust of the flesh, and the pride of life. "You will not die. You will fulfill your desire. Take that drug, enjoy that experience, earn that fame, etc. You'll be like God, determining what's good and evil and rule over your own life."

The sad fact is that Eve and Adam were ALREADY like God. They were created in His image. They had princely dominion over the earth and over the creep that crawled into their garden. They reflected the light of God's glory (Psalm 8: 5). Eve was tempted to become something that she *already was*.

She believed a lie that maybe God was withholding something good from her and ate from the tree of knowledge of good and evil.

The garment of light surrounding Adam and Eve and the crown of dominion both disappeared (Psalm 8). For the first time, shame entered the Garden. Spiritual death happened, even though their physical bodies lived on for 930 years.

Who told them they were naked? Who told them they were now shameful creatures? Not God. He made a covering for them and took away their shame. That's what He is about.

Believers, you are no longer naked. You, who are born again of the Spirit, are clothed with the very righteousness of God in Christ. First Peter says, by His stripes you are healed. Sure, you don't always feel like it or act like it. But that is your legal position in the kingdom of Light.

Faith says what God says. Write 2 Cor. 5: 17 in your prayer journal. The mind is not yet new and the physical body will not be made new until the resurrection, but the spirit man inside you is now a totally new creation made to have fellowship with the Father.

Example prayer:

Father, You made garments of skin by shedding the blood of an animal to cover the nakedness of Adam and Eve after they lost their garments of light (Gen. 3: 21). Thank You that Jesus has given us a new garment of righteousness, paid for with His sinless blood. In Him, I no longer have any condemnation according to Romans 8: 1. Thank you that I am redeemed from the curse of the law and by His stripes I am healed. Amen.

†

True Wisdom Has Two Sides

This is what the Lord quickened to my heart this morning. True wisdom has two sides (Job 11: 6). A natural side and a supernatural side. During a visitation from the Lord, Sara heard she was going to have a baby. In the natural, she had never seen a 90-yr.-old woman give birth. She laughed at the possibility. Yet she was about to enter the supernatural world through the prophetic word of God.

When Jesus ministered in Israel, He wept over the hardened hearts of people who did not recognize the day of their visitation (Luke 19:42). The heart of the Lord is grieved by the laughter of unbelief, which walks only by sight in the natural realm. Faith is the evidence of things not seen.

We have supernatural promises for divine health in God's word. Yet most of us tend to remain only in the natural realm when it comes to fighting disease. When we begin to renew our minds to receive supernatural health, how do we keep the experiences of others, who failed to receive, from shaking our faith? How do we deal with lingering symptoms in our own bodies?

We do it by applying the lessons we learn from Job and do not trust in our own righteousness. There are hidden things that we don't know (Deut. 29: 29) but we hold fast to the truth that we *do* know (Heb. 10: 23).

The things that **are revealed** belong to us and to our children. We learn from Joshua, that there are giants in the promised land to be conquered. The promises of God are our promised land. We learn to be skillful in using the "weapons of our warfare" to defeat those giants.

We do it by asking the question: who told you that God's word won't work for you? We recognize the lie when we hold it up to the light of Truth, pure truth. Jesus said God's Word is truth, unchanging, settled forever in heaven. He is Jehovah Rapha, the God Who heals.

If the illness does not diminish over time, we go to the throne of grace and ask the Holy Spirit to give us supernatural wisdom (James 1: 5).

"In the thirty-ninth year of his reign Asa was afflicted with a disease in his feet. Though his disease was severe, even in his illness he did not seek help from the LORD, but only from the physicians." (2 Chron. 16: 12).

There is nothing wrong with seeking help from physicians. Doctors are certainly one of God's chosen healing-delivery systems. However, the Lord is pleased when we seek Him *first*, according to Matt. 6:33-34. He wants us to come to Him for healing. Faith says what God says.

Example prayer:

Father I am seeking You as my Great Physician. You said I will find. I am knocking. You said the door will be opened. According to Your Word, I have healing in the atonement. I thank you for supernatural wisdom to learn how to receive it. Amen.

Testimony:

On Thursday, Jan 11, 2018 at 4:29 I sent a message to our support group.

Precious Believers who are standing in prayer with us: Here's what happened on January 11 of 2018. Husband John was still weak and shaky, almost two weeks after he suffered a violent reaction to chemotherapy for esophageal cancer. He had not been eating much at all. I wasn't sure I could load him in the car for his radiation treatment, so I called to borrow a walker from a neighbor. Then I walked outside and said, "Lord, I have done what I can. If there is anything I need to do, show me. Please give me **supernatural wisdom**.

I felt these words rise up in my spirit: "Go lay your hands on him and speak strength into his body." I faltered. What if nothing happens? Will he lose all faith in prayer, since he seems to be struggling with faith in healing? Doubt can rob us of the boldness to pray.

Then I seemed to hear these words: "But what if

something does happen?" So, I did what I felt the holy Spirit prompted.

John got out of bed at once, ate and began to lose all tremors and shakiness. He even wanted a chopped beef barbecue for lunch and got most of it down. He did not need the walker to go to the Cancer Center. Today he is even better and eating well even while wearing the chemo infusion pack.

That January day, I saw a definite turn-around. John suffered no more collapses. In spite of four more treatments of toxic chemo, he did not have another reaction. His appetite and his strength continued to improve.

In April of 2018, all scans, scopes, and tests came back showing my John is free of cancer. Praise God who watches over His word to perform it. Cancer does not lord it over us. Jesus is Lord over cancer. Amen.

Faith says what God says. His words are treasures to strengthen and equip you. Personalize those verses which speak to your situation or condition.

Example Prayer:

"I would have lost heart, unless I had believed that I would see the goodness of the LORD in the land of the living. Your promises strengthen me and I am of good courage while I wait on You, Lord." (Psa. 27: 13-14). Amen.

†

Greater Than I Imagined

When the Lord dropped this powerful truth into my mind I just said, *Wow*. It's so simple and yet so profound. Think about this. The blood of lamb spread on the door posts and lintels of the Hebrews was powerful enough to keep the angel of death out for every family in Egypt.

How much greater and more powerful is the blood of the perfect Lamb of God, Jesus. His blood applied to the doorposts and lintels of our spiritual heart can stop the angel of death at the door. No illness, which is the beginning of death, can cross the bloodline.

Are you thinking that applies only to the spirit of man? That is what we've been taught in so many traditional churches. However, Psalm 105: 37 says there was not one sick or feeble among them when they left Egypt. Think about this. Their physical bodies were healed by that blood, while a plague of death raged all around them on the night of the Passover. Not one Egyptian family was spared the loss of a first born.

There were about 600,000 men on foot (Ex. 12: 37) besides women and children. All left Egypt in perfect health. God needed an army of strong soldiers to defeat the enemies in the promised land. He still does. Why would He strike his army with any sickness or disease? The answer is, He would not. He struck the body of

Jesus and His perfect blood has not lost its power. We are healed by His stripes. We need only to receive it by faith like the woman with the issue of blood whose faith drew healing from the Lord into her body (Mark 5: 34). When we renew our minds to this truth, healing is on the way.

Amen!!!

†

The Gift Of Language

Animals don't have it. We will never sit down and have a theological discussion with a cat or a dog, or a horse. Well, maybe with a donkey (Numbers 22: 28). Yes, animals do communicate. I can almost hear what my cat has to say to me about his food. But only man created in the image of God has the ability to speak, write, compose and use the gift of language. As I ponder this, I am in awe of the power of words.

A brief glance at the book of Proverbs, underlining verses regarding speech, and the reader cannot help but be impressed. Words spoken by the Father created everything we see in the universe. We are made from the Word of God. Speaking His words from a believing heart over our bodies and our circumstances cannot help but produce change within the realm of our authority.

What an awesome thought. Our words have power. How often do we use that power, speaking negative, doubt filled, hopeless words? Our lives are shaped by what we believe in our hearts and speak with our mouths, according to Mark 11: 23-25. Think about what you might have said in the past that is happening in your life today, good or bad.

We worship a Heavenly Father, who speaks to us. Jesus said the sheep know their shepherd's voice. If we aren't hearing that voice, it's time to get into God's word and learn how. Our prayers should not be monologues, which mine often are. But they should be conversations, allowing God to speak to us.

If I heard an audible voice, I'd probably fall over in a faint. However, I have heard the voice of the Spirit speaking to my spirit and bringing to my remembrance what He reveals in scripture. I have the power and authority to speak God's Word! You do too.

Hear His Word, believe it, speak it, and watch it change your life.

†

Tormented By Guilt?

What is the image we have of ourselves? Oswald Chambers comments, "The root of all sin is the suspicion that God is not good." That's what the serpent told Eve. That God did not want her to enjoy the delicious fruit of determining for herself what is good and evil. What a bitter price for that choice. Eve knew shame and guilt for the first time. She lost her image of being created to reflect the very glory of God.

Once he snares someone, the accuser brings remembrance of past sin to make a person feel he is unworthy of God's blessing. That's what he did to Joseph's brothers. Even after Joseph forgave them and settled them in the best land of Egypt, they worried that he might take vengeance on them after their father Jacob died. Joseph's great mercy in his dealings with his eleven brothers is a type of Jesus blotting out our transgressions and remembering them no more.

His half-brothers had wanted to kill him, just as Christ's own Jewish people demanded his death. Here is a great truth: They meant it for bad, but the Father used this great offense "to preserve the lives of many people" (Gen. 50: 20). The Jews crucified Jesus and meant it for bad, but God used that event to preserve the lives of many people. He has reserved the best blessings for His people, even though they do nothing to deserve it. Joseph prepared a place for his unworthy people and gave them the best of the land in Egypt. Jesus has been preparing a place for us, the best place, even though we also have done nothing worthy of His blessing.

Example Prayer:

Father, 1 give You all honor, praise and thanksgiving for preserving my life. You do not withhold Your best blessings from me, even when I feel so unworthy. I am made worthy by the blood of Christ which cleanses all my unrighteousness. That blood never loses its power and makes me to overcome my guilt. Since You do not remember it, why should I? Take that, Satan! My new image in the Word is this: I am blessed, healed, and more than a conqueror. Amen.

†

The Whole Creation Groans

The wages of sin are death. We usually assume that sin leads to sickness and actually, diseases are the beginnings of death. I just spent an hour at our veterinarian's office where I watched people bring their diseased and suffering pets. Some dogs were arthritic. Some cats had various forms of cancers. Other pets suffered allergies, eating disorders, and age-related infirmities.

Tell me, what sin did these dogs and cats commit to be stricken so? Animals cannot tell a lie, commit adultery, cheat, envy. The animal members of God's creation are not subject to the higher moral law which humans are held accountable to. These pets suffer simply because of the original curse brought on by Adam.

Rom. 8: 19-22 says, all of creation groans ""*For the creation was subjected to futility, not willingly, **but because of Him** who subjected it in hope; because the creation itself also will be delivered from the bondage of corruption into the glorious liberty of the children of God."*

<u>*Romans 8:20-21 NKJV*</u>

. . . For the creation was subjected to futility (death), not willingly, and all creation groans in hope that the creation itself will be set free from its bondage to corruption (suffering and death) and obtain the freedom of the glory of the children of God.

Wrong thinking can rob a believer of his right to divine healing, simply because he has been taught that disease was brought on by his sin, when in fact it is because of Adam's sin. Certainly, unhealthy and sinful lifestyles can lead to various diseases. However, after repentance and forgiveness (Matt. 9:5), the sincere believer has every right to healing provided by the stripes of Jesus in I Peter 2: 24. Good news. Jesus came to redeem us, spirit, soul, and body. Sin is never greater than grace.

Example Prayer:

Father, You said I would know the truth and the truth sets me free. I have learned that righteousness is not something I do. It is something that I am, because of Christ's imputing it to me. Therefore, sickness has no power over me. Jesus is Lord over sickness. I am free. Amen.

†

The Evil-Voice That Spoke In The Night

September 3, 1982
Wichita, KS

I wakened from a nightmare in which I was suffering from a painful stabbing sensation in my right breast. Somewhat shaken by the sensation, I thought to myself, "I'm glad that was only a dream."

However, it was *more than a dream*. The stabbing pain persisted like a hot needle piercing my flesh. Instantly I began to encourage myself in the Lord's healing words. I knew I had exercised faith for my 5-yr.-old daughter's complete healing from tonsillitis on the day she was scheduled for possible surgery.

Now as I lay there in the dark at approximately 2:30 a.m., hurting for no apparent reason, I heard an evil, sneering voice speak to my mind. "You are going to have cancer. You are going to need surgery." The voice spoke in a mocking tone. "Where is your faith now?"

Previously, I had given little thought to what the Bible calls the kingdom of darkness. I was too college educated and had dismissed evil spirits as mostly superstition. However, there was in inward awareness, and absolute conviction that I was hearing from an evil spirit at that moment. My heart started to pound.

I began to answer out loud. "My faith is in the Word

of the Lord and He has redeemed me from the curse of the law. I do not accept this pain. I refuse it in the Name of Jesus, so you can take your lying symptoms and get out! I resist you in Jesus' name. Father I thank You that Your word is true and that my righteousness is from You and I'm covered and cleansed by the Blood of the Lamb."

I continued to praise and thank the Lord, rising from the bed to stand by the window, praying in the spirit and in English. The stabbing pain seemed to lessen somewhat.

I crawled back into bed and slept without fear, but the pain persisted intermittently. Morning came and I went to teach my classes at Bethel Life School, feeling fatigued and listless.

Like what happened to Job, who said, "the thing I feared has come upon me," I wondered if I had opened a door to evil by fear. Years before, I had read a Reader's Digest article titled "The Disease Women Fear" about breast cancer when I was just a teenager. Those words describing the disease kept rising up. I prayed inwardly.

The stabbing pain gradually became less and less frequent as the day progressed. Because the dream voice was so unusually vivid and the pain so real, I wrote down the experience on the back of my daily bulletin and stuck it inside my Bible. By noon of that day, I felt no more pain.

Eleven years later on July 10, 1993 (my birthday) I was diagnosed with a small, tumor. It had actually been present on my baseline mammogram **from three years**

before. The radiologist had missed it. However, I knew it had actually been in my body since September of 1982 when the demonic entity attacked me. God did not permit it to grow, even though I had been on hormone replacement for three years, (1990 to 93) which doctors believe will cause some breast cancers to grow.

The biopsy to determine the diagnosis was conducted by a long needle which was inserted in *exactly the same location* as the needle-sharp stabbing-pain I had experienced on the night of the dream. I did not think of it at that moment.

On September 1, 1993, I underwent a bi-lateral mastectomy. If I had known then what I know today, my authority in Christ, I doubt that I would have had that surgery. However, overwhelmed by a series of tragic events that swept over my family like a tsunami, wave after wave at the time, I lost focus.

About three months after the surgery, I opened my now-worn-and-tattered Bible, which had been replaced by a new one. There was the long-forgotten school bulletin describing the nightmare. That's when I knew that even through the surgery, God is so very faithful.

Example Prayer:

"Yes, there is one who is evil and mighty, the thief who comes to steal, kill, and destroy, (John 10: 10) but God is mightier. He sent His Son, *that we might have life and that more abundantly.*"

†

May God Open Your Eyes

May God open your eyes to question the lies which your mind believes.

Who told you Jesus isn't the same today as yesterday? That He no longer heals people by His Word? that He won't bless us if we aren't completely deserving? That the blessings of God's kingdom are only to be experienced after we die? Or even that He also causes tribulation to punish and perfect us?

These are lies I once believed. They are not supported by New Testament scripture. They make the Word of none effect and keep us from the full blessing, which Jesus has provided in John 10: 10. Jesus is not the author of sickness and death. He is the author of life.

Just imagine the following scenario.

"The Lord appointed seventy-two others and sent them two by two ahead .. He told them, 'The harvest is plentiful, but the workers are few ... 'Heal the sick who are there and tell them, The kingdom of God is near you' " (Luke 10:9).

Peter and Thomas have their marching orders. They are preaching about the Kingdom of God in a village where they meet a crippled beggar. Peter asks, "Sir, do you want to be healed?"

The fellow nods his head hopefully, and then adds, "But I am unworthy. I'm a sinner."

Thomas looks at Peter doubtfully: "I know the Lord gave us authority to heal in His Name. But what if it's not God's will to heal this man? Maybe he needs to repent. Shouldn't we ask, *Father if it be Thy will, please heal this sinner?"*

Peter is astonished. "Come on Tom! Jesus *already told us to heal* the sick. Therefore, it IS His will, dummy. He didn't say we should ask them to repent first. Did you ever hear Jesus, even one time ask, *Father is it Your will for this person to be made whole?"*

Thomas agrees. "You're right. We should pray, but what if nothing happens?"

"We've been walking with Jesus for nearly three years now. He showed us how to heal the sick. Yeah, there was that time when He couldn't do any mighty works in His own hometown because of their unbelief, but that didn't stop Him from going on to heal the sick everywhere else. That shouldn't stop us from obeying His command. We imitate the way He does it. Just like this." Turning to the cripple, Peter says, "I see you are a beggar. Silver and gold we have none, but such as we have we give to you. In the name of Jesus Christ, the Messiah, rise up and walk!"

The pair watch in awe when the beggar slowly rises to his feet. At first his legs wobble, then he takes a few haltering steps. Soon he is leaping and walking and praising God. And so are Peter and Thomas. (Actually, it was Peter and John in the book of Acts 3: 5. I used Thomas as the character in this fictional story to make a point.)

I know what you're thinking. That kind of authority was for the apostles only. Think again. Jesus said these signs will follow *them that believe* (Mark 16: 17-18). That's you and me.

†

My Will, God's Will, Or Satan's?

"I am willing. Be whole." (Luke 5: 13)

We've all heard it said. Often after some kind of tragedy or natural disaster. Even at funerals. "God must have needed this young person, so He took him. God's will be done."

The words sound so very pious. Jesus said it in the Lord's prayer. "Thy will be done . . ." however many people ignore the best part, "on earth as it is in Heaven." There are no deaths, no tragedies, no disasters in Heaven. No tornadoes. No genetic malfunctions. No plagues. Clearly God's will is NOT being done on earth as it in Heaven. Not yet.

Who told me the lie that everything happening must be God's will? If I believe that, I will not resist those things that He told me to resist. That is spiritual apathy. It is choosing not to exercise my God-given authority over the enemy and allowing him to steal, kill, and destroy me and people around me (John 10: 10). It's a believer who has the full armor of God and never puts it on—never wields the sword of the spirit against the adversary (Luke 10: 19).

Authority you do not use is victory you will not have. That's not to say we win every battle. Some things just happen outside our realm of authority, or we simply do not have enough revelation on how to win.

People perish through ignorance of the word (Hosea 4: 6).

Then there are the things that are revealed (Deut. 29: 29). Revealing your realm of authority, the weapons of spiritual warfare, and when and how to become skillful with them—that's what the meditations in this book are about.

Faith says what God says. Write 2 Cor. 10: 4 and Ephesians 6: 17 in your journal.

Example prayer:

Father in Heaven, show me my realm of authority. Teach me when to take up the sword of the Spirit so that the enemy's will is not done. Teach me when to lay down my will so that Your will may be done. Give me wisdom to know the difference. I ask for boldness to recognize and defeat Satan's works, both in my life and the lives of others. I believe I receive this boldness. Amen.

†

Wait And See?

When I first began to believe that God wants us to pray for the sick, I was too timid to pray anywhere but in private. Then I would wait to see what happened. Only if a recovery happened would I tell the person that I had prayed. Beloved, that is NOT faith.

Faith is voice-activated and always believes **before** receiving the answer (Mark 11: 23-24). It's little wonder that no sick person I prayed for in private ever recovered immediately. Many never recovered at all.

So, what was I doing wrong?

I asked the Lord to show me. Is it my lack of faith, Lord? No, it's your lack of knowledge. There is a key of knowledge that opens Kingdom blessings (Luke 11: 52).

I began to study. Over the next several years, I learned the key of authority, the key of meditation, the key of Light, the difference between unbelief and little faith, and what the prayer of faith is not.

I also learned that Jesus asks us to minister to the sick and believe whether *or not* we see healing come.

In Jesus' home town of Nazareth, even He could do no mighty works there because of their unbelief. But that didn't stop Him from healing the sick everywhere else.

I believe in following His example. Just do it and stop hesitating. I have begun to see more people get healed, both instantly and gradually, by praying what God says over them.

The more a believer steps out and prays for people, the more healing they will see. And the opposite is also true. If you are too timid to pray a prayer of faith (authority) over the sick, then you will likely not see a healing.

Testimony from a young woman:

"My baby's ultrasound showed a hole in the wall of her heart. Harriett took my hands in hers, prayed for my baby, and also for my insurance to quit stalling the echo test. Just one hour later, my insurance company called and agreed to the test! Two weeks later, my doctor compared the second ultrasound to the first one. The hole in my baby's heart appeared clearly on the first ultrasound. On the next one, it had completely healed. That's when I knew what her middle name would be. It's Faith. She was born a healthy and beautiful baby in January, 2018 in Springfield, Missouri." – K.

†

A Begging Prayer Or A Prayer Of Authority?

In Numbers 12:13, When Miriam was stricken with leprosy, Moses cried out, "Heal her, O god. Heal her now I beseech Thee." This is a **begging prayer**. This is what most believers are taught to pray and do pray. I have prayed this way for years without seeing much victory.

Then I learned an amazing kingdom law, the law of the Spirit of life in Christ Jesus which sets us free from the law of sin and death (Rom. 8: 2).

Moses had to pray based on the law of blessing and cursing found in Deuteronomy 28. Miriam had brought herself under the curse of the law by her disobedience.

Then something wonderful happened. Jesus brought a new and better covenant to us by the cross.

The Lord impressed me to study how Jesus and the apostles dealt with illness. I found they NEVER prayed a begging prayer for healing. You won't find one example. They simply commanded by the **authority of Jesus' Name:** "Be healed. Take up your bed. Walk." This is the prayer of authority based on the fulfillment of the law, which Christ accomplished at Calvary (Rom. 8: 1-2). He set us free from the curse of the law, (Gal. 3: 13; I Pet. 2: 24; Luke 10: 19).

Below are two examples:

A begging prayer: "Father, we ask you to please heal this disease *if it be your will.*" That is a prayer of doubt—not faith—in the light of Jesus' own command to heal the sick (Matt. 10: 8). It assumes that healing may not always be the will of God. Doubt is usually based on experience or on wrong believing. It carries with it the assumption that we might not be worthy of healing. Again, ask yourself who told you that?

A prayer of Authority: "By the authority of Jesus (Luke 10: 19), and the power of His Blood I speak *to* the BODY and command it to be normal. I say in the name of Jesus, sickness does not lord it over me (or the person's name). Jesus is Lord over sickness. All glory and praise to God. Amen. ***Faith says what God says.***

Write Luke 10: 19 in your journal and begin to speak it over your life.

✝

What Seeds Produce The Harvest?

The parable of the sower is multi-layered with meaning. Jesus called it foundational to understand how the kingdom of God works in this world of which Satan is prince. I used to think the sower was the preacher and that is true. A more personal meaning is this: The seed is the word a believer plants in the good soil of his own heart.

There are a total of forty-four verses in the New Testament where the Greek word "sperma" is translated "seed." This is the same word from which we derive our English word "sperm."

To conceive and reap the harvest of health, you must first plant God's Words on healing like a seed in your heart. **Conception cannot take place without first planting the seed. And the more seed you plant, the greater the harvest. He who sows sparingly shall also reap sparingly.**

Faith only comes one way, by hearing and meditating on the Word (Rom 10: 17). "Christians who pray and believe for God's intervention but remain frustrated with the results often are missing the seeds of conception," according to Andrew Wommack. They don't know God's word, or they hear it once and allow the fowls of the air (doubt) to steal it. Or they lose their harvest by allowing cares of this world to occupy their time and simply neglect the word.

Faith says what God says. Words are seeds and seeds produce like things. Like produces like, each after its own kind (Gen. 1: 11). What seeds are you planting and speaking over your life? Ask yourself, am I agreeing with the enemy or with God? What harvest are you reaping?

Example prayer:

Lord, in Exodus 23:25, You said, "I will take sickness away from the midst of you." I speak this promise to my body in Jesus' Name. As I meditate on this word, I am sowing it into the good soil of my heart. I thank You that Your Word is incorruptible seed and never fails, so I am looking for a harvest of health. Amen.

†

They Spoke Faith Words

"The rock of my strength, my refuge is in God. Trust in Him at all times, oh people; *Pour out* your heart before Him; God is a refuge for us." --Psalm 62: 8.

I woke up this morning with this on my heart. Whenever King David poured out his heart before God, He usually ended his petition by calling the answer an *accomplished fact* before any circumstances changed. He named the problem or the enemy and voiced his complaint, but he almost never finished a psalm without declaring the victory and praising God for the answer— BEFORE he saw the answer. That's faith-talk. In the above scripture, he reminds himself that God is a refuge for us.

David **shouted** he would cut off Goliath's head, even without a sword in his hand (I Sam. 17: 46). The sword of the Spirit was in his mouth. David spoke the victory *before* he slung the first stone. That's declaring the end from the beginning. Then he used Goliath's own sword to sever his head.

Many people criticize the faith-talk teachers. However, every biblical hero spoke faith words and declared the end of the matter, like God does, *before it became a reality* in the natural world. Isaiah 46: 10 says God declares the end from the beginning. Consider the words of Abraham, Job, the Shunamite woman. Look at the prophets, who for hundreds of years declared the life and death of Jesus as though it was *already* done instead of in the far distant future. Jonah declared the Lord had brought him up from the depths (Jonah 2: 6) while he was STILL inside the whale's belly. Jonah was calling those things that were not yet in existence as though they were (Rom. 4: 17). **Faith says what God says.**

Write Luke 1: 37 and Phil. 4: 13 as your personal faith-seed words and speak them over your life.

†

Speaking A Blessing Or A Curse?

The answer to that question may surprise you. A blessing is any good thing you are speaking that you wish to come to pass. Life and death are in the power of the tongue (Prov.18: 21).

A curse is anything you speak that you *don't want* to come to pass. Not just things you damn. Things you inadvertently criticize. Hateful, negative words. Words like "stupid, idiot, fool."

Pastor John Kilpatrick was disappointed when he added a new $40,000 orchestra pit to his Brownsville church in Pensacola and it remained empty. He said, "I started calling it, you stupid hole. You $40, 000 hole. I cried out to God, Lord, there's no playing in the orchestra pit. God rebuked me. He simply said, *Stop cursing it*. I didn't cuss, but I suddenly realized I was cursing the pit with my negative words. I had to repent, stop it, and renounce my words."

Ugly words actually grieve the Holy Spirit according to Ephesians 4: 30-31. The atmosphere in your home changes, because He is grieved. How can He bring fullness of blessing where the atmosphere is defiled? We ask God to bless our day. Then we go around asking God to damn things whenever we get frustrated.

Speaking gentle words, pleasant words are "honey from the honeycomb, sweet to the soul and healing to the bones," (Prov. 16: 24). Our souls are encouraged when we hear positive and kind words spoken over us.

Bitter words do damage. "Your own soul is nourished when you speak kindly. You destroy yourself when you are cruel." (Prov. 11: 17).

By the way, after his words changed from negative, Pastor Kilpatrick's orchestra pit was soon filled with musicians. Words have power.

Example Prayer:

Father set a watch at the door of my mouth. May my words always be seasoned with grace, kindness, and truth. May I speak faith in agreement with Your words all the days of my life. Amen.

†

A life That Never fulfills God's purpose?

Sadly, there are those passive believers who sit back and wait for God to do something about their circumstances. They talk to God about the mountain instead of talking to the mountain about God. They are like sails hanging limply on the mast.

A sail is designed to catch the wind and propel a craft on the water. Without the wind, it does not fulfill its purpose.

The very breath of God, the rushing, mighty wind described in Acts 2: 2 filled 120 believers who had gathered in the upper room to wait for the promised Holy Spirit. From that day forward, their lives impacted the course of history and turned the world upside down.

The promise of the Holy Spirit is to every believer (Acts 2: 39). He "fills the sails" of believing hearts to do the works God has appointed them to do, (Eph. 2: 8-10).

The wonderful thing is there is no need to wait. Since Pentecost, the Holy Spirit is already here to be poured out on those who *ask* Him (Luke 11: 13).

Jesus promised this gift of power to become witnesses to the fact that Jesus is living (Acts 1: 8). Now we have something to talk about. That amazing reality burns within us to tell all the world. We are no longer empty sails.

Example Prayer:

Father, I thank You for the gift of the Holy Spirit. He is my comforter, my guide, my teacher, and He brings to my remembrance the words You have spoken (John 14 and 15). Fill me daily to impact the lives of those who do not know about this unspeakable joy. Amen.

†

Genesis Is A Template

Do you doubt it is God's will to bless His children? Jesus said it is the Father's good pleasure to give us the kingdom, (Luke 12: 32). Yet so many have a fear of being punished instead of blessed.

Here's what the Lord laid on my heart today. When God created Adam and Eve, He **blessed** them (Genesis 1: 28). His blessing included dominion and a fruitful life on every level.

What did they do to earn His blessing? Absolutely *nothing*. That is a most profound revelation when you realize that Genesis is a template for what happens in the New Testament.

The first couple were already blessed beyond anything the deceiver could offer them.

Then something terrible happened. Adam broke covenant with God (Hosea 6: 7).

As I look at the blessings listed in Deuteronomy 28, I see the words "If you," repeated. "If you hearken. If you obey." The blessings of the Mosaic Covenant were all conditional upon *you* and *your* performance. If you couldn't keep all the various laws—and no one could—you lost the blessings.

Then something wonderful happened. The cross. A new and better covenant.

The focus is no longer on you. It is entirely on Jesus.

Because of the cross, we do not have to *do* anything to earn God's blessing. We are blessed as Adam and Eve were blessed. Simply by becoming God's children (John 1: 12).

Except one thing, and this is important! We must resist the deceiver, who tries to rob us of those blessings, just like he robbed Adam and Eve. **Faith says what God says.**

Write Genesis 1: 28 and John 1: 12 and begin speak these verses over your life.

†

A Supernatural Harvest

There is something almost supernatural about light. Light is transmitted through the air all around us. We can see images of historical events, people from the past, and current happenings on TV. A newscaster can appear everywhere simultaneously. Compare this simultaneous TV image to the ever-present Spirit of God. The Holy Spirit is in every believer at the same time. That's why Jesus said it is expedient for Him to go away. Thankfully, He did not leave us at the mercy of the god of this world.

When I began to study Revelation, I saw chaos and darkness at the end of time. I heard the Spirit say, "To understand the end, you must go back to the beginning." Wow. Of course! God declared the end from the beginning. He spoke Light into existence. Light defeated darkness and chaos in the beginning. And Light will defeat chaos and darkness at the end.

Isaiah 9: 3 says, ". . . for those living in the land of deep **darkness** a light ***has dawned***." You're thinking of that little light bulb that goes on when someone "gets" the message. But have you ever thought about the two invisible kingdoms here on earth (Col. 1: 13)? One is a kingdom of darkness and the other of Light.

Now I'm going to mess with your minds if you're thinking natural science. In verse three of Genesis, God said, "Let there be light." Light came into existence and overcame the darkness. This is a picture of the Kingdom of Light overcoming the kingdom of darkness (Acts 16: 18). We also had both day and night.

That is astonishing when you discover that the natural SUN was not even created until the fourth Day. Yet on the third day in verse eleven, the earth begins *to bloom and blossom and bring forth fruit.* How can this be? Even without the sun?

Because Jesus is the Light of the world, He brought forth a supernatural harvest in the supernatural Son light. That is what He wants believers to do. **Faith says what God says.**

Write a verse in your prayer journal which describes the supernatural harvest you are looking for. When the enemy tells you it isn't happening, remind him that God's word does not return to Him empty.

†

No Darkness In Heaven?

"For once you were darkness, but now you are light in the Lord. Walk as children of light," Ephesians 5:8.

The Hubble telescope shows myriads of galaxies, even when aimed toward what was once thought to be only darkness. It seems the universe is full of darkness, but when God said, "Let there be light," the light shone. As we see on the previous page, the first light was *supernatural Light* (Gen. 1: 3).

Darkness and chaos were here on the earth. The Hebrew word In Genesis, *tohu va-bohu,* means something like 'desolate and waste', describing the disorderly and functionless chaos. However, God does not create chaos (I Cor. 14: 33). Satan does.

Even before He created the sun, God spoke, and the supernatural Light of the world began to overcome the darkness. This is a picture of Jesus defeating the evil one.

After Satan and his kingdom of darkness are finally defeated and the city of God comes to earth, there will be "no more need for lamps, sun, or moon, for the glory of God will shine on us," (Rev. 22:5).

This is an amazing statement and certainly defies everything we know about the laws of physics and natural science.

Jesus is the source of Supernatural Light. Until then, He has given us His authority to overcome the darkness (Col. 1: 13) here in the earth *where we need it*. There is no darkness to overcome in heaven. **Faith says what God says.**

Write John 8: 12 in your journal. Speak this verse over your life.

†

Which Light Do You Walk in?

When I studied the kingdom of God, a spiritual kingdom of Light, not yet fully manifest on earth as it is in Heaven, I found that this kingdom is already inside the believers (John 5:24). We who believe have already passed from darkness to light. We have a choice to walk in natural sun light and also in supernatural Son light (Rev. 22: 5).

If we walk only by natural light, we will only have natural results. This does not mean that we refuse sound medical treatment. If we take medication, we thank God for it and ask for supernatural results as well. Dave Walker, a practicing physician and author of the book ***God in the ICU****,* notes that if an enormously fat person develops a backache and asks for healing, but does nothing about her weight problem, it is unlikely that she will be healed. God desires our cooperation in the healing process. Dr. Walker says there are other issues that may block healing, and this prompts him to ask God if that is the case when praying, and it also allows him "to continue to know that God wants us healed."

Obviously, doctors are limited in what they can do.

The kingdom of darkness is a reality. That is why we have tribulation in this world. But be of good cheer. Jesus has overcome the world, and as members of His body on earth we are equipped to overcome also.

God tests, but He does not tempt us. Some people teach that tribulation is from God (and it does perfect patience) but we are not to bow down to it. We are to overcome it. If it were from God, why would He want us to overcome it? It may take a while, but we are created for victory, not defeat.

How do we overcome? Not by begging God to do what He has equipped us to do. By the blood of the Lamb and the word of our testimony (Rev. 12: 11). **Faith says what God says.**

Write Psalm 119: 105 and Eph. 1: 18.

Example prayer:

Holy Spirit, fill my eyes with the Light which comes from understanding Your word. Enlighten the eyes of my heart. Strengthen my inner being so that I am walking in the spirit and not after the flesh. Amen.

✝

Words From The Heart

Out of the heart the mouth speaks. That is why you must guard your heart with all diligence. If you want supernatural Son Light and a supernatural harvest, you must plant God's Word in your heart, and speak it over whatever needs to be changed. Faith says what God says. Your words have power.

Do not continually say things such as, "I'll never get over this. My arthritis is killing me. I'll never get ahead. I'll never be able to pay off all this debt." Who told you that? Why, the devil of course.

Start by drawing near to God. Blessing Him. Seeking Him first for Who He is, and not for what He can do for you. Then change those negative natural words to what God says: "I am an overcomer. I overcome by the blood of the Lamb and the word of my testimony. I had almost lost hope unless I believed I would see the goodness of the Lord in the land of the living. I am confident of this." Psalm 27: 13. That's walking by supernatural Son Light.

You might not see big changes overnight, but stay consistent according to James 1: 7. A double-minded man doubts and will not receive anything from the Lord.

This is not something you "try" for a while and then toss it aside and go back to begging God because you decide it's not working. I have learned that by firsthand experience.

This is a commitment to plant the word-seed deep in the good soil of your heart and water it every day. Like the farmer watches for a crop, you will see first the blade, then the leaves, then the full grain. You will reap a harvest.

A crop failure only happens when a person is not consistent and gives more attention to the natural circumstances than to the Word of God. **Faith says what God says.**

Write Joshua 1: 8 and be a doer of the word.

†

Authority You Do Not Use Is Victory You Will Not Have

I used to think God postponed Adam's death on the day he sinned. Actually, his physical body lived on for a total of 930 years, but his oneness with the Father was broken with that first bite. That is spiritual death—separation from the Father. Adam also lost his crown of dominion (Psalm 8:5-6). He lost his garment of light, (Psalm 104: 2; Isa. 61:10;). He was naked and ashamed. From that day on, mankind has been born separated from the Father and born **spiritually dead** (Col. 2:13; Eph. 2: 1-3).

When we receive Christ, we are spiritually reborn because of His perfect blood, which legally satisfied Heaven's demand for justice. God becomes our spiritual Father (Heb. 12:9). Not only are we cleansed of all unrighteousness, **we get back our garment of light (Christ's robe of righteousness, Isa. 61:10), we also get back our dominion--our authority over the god of this world who is called prince of** the power of the air now at work in the sons of disobedience (Luke 10:19).

Authority you do not use is victory you will not have. The first commandment was to be fruitful, multiply, and take **dominion** over the earth. Why would Adam have to take dominion over it? It was already His. He had the privilege of naming every living thing that creeps on the earth. When you name an animal it usually becomes your pet. The animals were not carnivorous at that time and no threat to him (Gen 1: 30).

So why take dominion? Think about it. Satan was already there in Eden. Adam had the legal right to command him to leave the garden (Gen. 1:26). All he had to do was say, "I have dominion over everything that lives and creeps on the ground. So, get out of here, you creep!" Sadly, Adam lost his dominion.

Testimony:

One spring a few years ago, my husband noticed our redbud tree was not blooming in the spring. Some branches were obviously dead and the rest of the tree looked sickly. My husband was ready to cut it down. However, I said we could speak to the tree and command it to live and not die, and it must obey us (Luke 17: 6). He mumbled, "Can we do this when nobody is looking?"

He talks to the TV, the car, and the computer among other things. How many of you talk to your hammer?

I reminded him that Jesus spoke to trees. Supernatural words control the natural world. (Genesis).

Well, we did speak life to that little tree. Guess what. That tree has been blooming and healthy every spring since then. You have the same authority to speak to your body and command it to live and not die. Start declaring, Jesus is Lord over sickness and disease. Sickness does not lord it over me. Amen.

Blinded To Natural Light

On the road to Damascus, Paul saw Jesus appear as a supernatural light, so brilliant it blinded him for three days (Acts 9: 2-4).

Interestingly, he was the ONLY one of the travelers who heard the voice of the Lord. The rest of them thought it was thunder.

Sometimes we have to become blind to the natural in order to see the supernatural light. We are body, soul, and spirit. Our natural eyes see only by natural sun light. Our spirit eyes see into the spirit world by faith in the Son's Light. Paul's natural eye sight was restored by Ananias, who also had been given a vision into the spirit world and was told where to find Paul.

I am not satisfied to see only what is natural in the world. I want eyes of faith to see all that Jesus makes possible and to do the greater works He has appointed to His followers. I cannot do that if I am ill.

Example prayer:

Father, I put you in remembrance of Your word as you instructed me to do. I choose to give your Word final authority over the reports of the doctors or symptoms which say there is disease in this body. Blind my eyes to those reports. I choose to look to

Faith Says What God Says by Harriett Ford

Your Word which says in Romans 3:4, "Let God be true and every man a liar." Whatever contradicts His eternal word is subject to change and cannot be eternal truth. This is not to say I will ignore sound medical advice. I will fight illness with both natural and supernatural wisdom, however I choose the Word as my final authority, over any other, in order to reap a supernatural harvest. Amen.

†

The Prayer Of Doubt

Many kinds of prayer are described in the New Testament. Prayers of agreement, petition, intercession, submission. These are only a few. It is important to note that only ONE type of prayer is named in the New Testament that heals:" the prayer of faith, shall *heal* the sick" according to James 5: 15.

As earlier stated, this is NOT a prayer of doubt, such as, "Lord, please heal, if it be Thy will." Yes, I have stated this before. I am a teacher, and teachers repeat their instructions. So does our Lord. Remember how Jesus says, "Truly, truly I say. . ."

Doubt assumes that God does not always want to heal the sick, contrary to what James is saying. The prayer of faith is not a begging prayer, asking God to change His mind and deliver the sick person. What good would that do if wasn't God's will and He had struck us with disease in the first place?

James teaches us that, yes, church people do get sick, however the prayer of faith will heal them and their sins will be forgiven. Many people don't like it when this is taught because it upsets their pet doctrines and false teaching that sickness is from God or that God is perfecting patience in us, or disciplining us. I have never found any basis for that teaching in the New Testament.

True, there are passages in the Old Testament which label disease as curses from God for disobedience. However, a careful study of Jesus' life shows that He came to redeem us from curses.

God permits disease because of the sin of Adam and because His people don't learn how to exercise their blood-bought dominion (Hos. 4: 6). Throughout the scriptures, God's will is that His children overcome all affliction (Psa. 34: 19). When we learn how to operate in the *law* of the Spirit of life in Christ, we are to become victorious over the law of sin and death. **Faith says what God says.**

Write Hosea 4: 6 and Psa. 34: 19. Find a New Testament prayer of authority spoken by Jesus or by the apostles. Write it out and make it your prayer model.

†

The Things That Are Revealed

When Jesus gave Peter the keys of the Kingdom He was speaking of **supernatural-revelation knowledge,** which is the solid rock foundation for building His body of believers.

Our Lord said, "Flesh and blood has not *revealed* this to you, but my Father who is in heaven." Knowing Who Jesus is, is an ongoing supernatural **revelation** (Eph. 1: 17-25). We do not know Him by natural knowledge. "No one knows who the Son is except the Father, and no one knows who the Father is except the Son and those to whom the Son chooses to **reveal** him," Luke 10: 22.

The keys of the Kingdom are spiritual laws that operate in the hearts and mouths of believers (Luke 11: 52; Rom 10: 8-10). The tongue sets spiritual laws in motion. When you speak faith-words, agreeing with God's Word, you get what you say, (Mark 11:23-24). But if you don't have the knowledge yet to say them, you are likely speaking doubt.

When you speak doubt-words, agreeing with the enemy, you get what you say (Numbers 14:28). Both death and life are in the **power of the tongue**, (Prv. 18:21; Rom. 10: 8-10). Are we speaking life or death over our circumstances? Are we acknowledging only the symptoms, or the Word that says we are more than conquerors? Words are the key to the kingdom of Light and also to the kingdom of darkness. **Faith says what God says.**

Write Proverbs 18: 21 here.

Example prayer:

Father, I thank you that even though my body may be showing signs of disease, You *reveal* in Your word that believers have the authority by the blood of the Lamb to deny its right to stay there. I command these symptoms to leave in Jesus' Name. I act by faith on the Word which says death and life are in the power of the tongue. Even though I may feel like going back to bed. I'm going to practice sound medical advice, but also act like God's Word is true, dress, and go about my daily schedule. Praise God.

Two Kinds Of Knowledge

Satan's tactic has always been to cast doubt on what God plainly says. In Eden, his deceitful words to Eve meant: "You do not need to follow God's way, for it is obviously unfair. You can follow your *own* way. You will not die. You can use your knowledge to decide what is good and what is evil. You can be like God in determining what is right and wrong."

Ever since then, man has rejected God's standard of righteousness in favor of making up his own. **The key to the knowledge of evil is rejecting God's knowledge.** This opens doors to societal acceptance of things which are clearly against God's will and leads to spiritual death. Beloved, we cannot allow society to form our morality when it contradicts God's word. The prophet Isaiah said, "If you do not stand firm in your faith, you will not stand at all" (Isa. 7: 9).

As earlier mentioned, there is a key of knowledge. Jesus promised it to Peter in Matt. 16: 19. **The key of knowledge of God's ways, which lead to spiritual life.** Jesus said in Luke 11: 52, *"Woe unto you, lawyers! for ye have taken away the **key of knowledge*** — Ye have obscured and destroyed the true knowledge of the Messiah (His coming and what His sacrifice truly means). By your wrong interpretations of Scripture, you have filled the people with strong prejudices against the gospel, so that you not only reject it yourselves, but hinder others from receiving it."

If you do not have the key of knowledge about God's kingdom and how it operates, you will be easily deceived.

Faith in God's word begins with hearing it, meditating on it, seeking the Holy Spirit's revelation of what it means. I promise you, this is the most exciting pursuit. Getting to know God's mind. **Faith says what God says.**

Write 1 Cor. 2: 16.

Example prayer:

Lord, I choose to renew my mind according to Your word and not according to what the world says is right or wrong. I have the mind of Christ as I meditate on Your Word and it becomes my standard for Truth. Amen.

Deliverance From All Affliction

Many Christians expect to endure afflictions, believing this is just part of life in a fallen world. Some even believe God has appointed them to His people.

The Bible does say, "Many are the afflictions of the righteous" (Psalm 34:19). However, this is only part of the truth. The rest of this scripture is, "But the Lord delivers him out of them all." People who blame God for "*afflictions*" have not learned the good part—deliverance!

The Lord is not causing the afflictions, or He would not be delivering us from *them ALL*. He is not a house divided against Himself.

However, deliverance is not automatic. Most often it takes a good fight of faith. A fight that doesn't even begin if a person thinks God is afflicting him to somehow perfect his faith. Why would we fight against God? **Faith says what God says.**

Write I Tim. 6: 12 and Heb. 10: 23 and begin to speak these verses over your life daily.

We Are Not Appointed to Wrath.

People often point to verses in the Old Testament which indicate that God brought plagues and affliction on people who violated the law. Certainly, He judged the earth during Noah's flood. He named curses and penalties for sin when the law was put into effect through Moses.

He is a God of judgment and justice. Without judgment, there is no justice. Then something happened. The cross.

Thanks be to Jesus, we see the Father is also a God of mercy. Because of Jesus fulfilling the penalty for sin, we have a "new and better covenant" (Heb. 8: 6). The cross speaks of God's righteousness, because He did not merely excuse sin. He judged it.

Many people do not consider that all God's wrath was poured out on Jesus. There is no wrath laid up for believers in Christ (I Thess. 5: 9). It would be redundant for God to lay the penalty for my sin on Jesus, and then appoint affliction and disease to me for those same sins. "Many are the afflictions of the righteous, but the Lord delivers him out of them all," (Psa. 34: 19). Plagues and affliction are never God's perfect will.

Here is a profound truth. God permits what people permit. Why? Because He gave man dominion over the earth (Psa. 8: 6). Adam gave up his dominion to Satan (2 Cor. 4: 4: John 12: 31). Christ gave His followers dominion once more (Luke 10: 19). When they learn to exercise their God-given authority, He acts through them to bring His will to pass. **Faith says what God says.**

Write Jeremiah 29: 11 here and speak it over your life.

†

Rightly Dividing The Word

The words "rightly divide" mean to cut a straight road. To avoid misunderstanding the character of God, one must separate the law of sin and death from the law of the Spirit of life in Christ Jesus (Rom 8: 2). For instance, in 2 Kings 1: 10, Elijah called down fire from heaven and consumed fifty men. So, as previously stated, we see a God whose character is to judge and punish. Without judgment, there is no justice, and God is a God of both.

In the New Testament, when the disciples asked Jesus, "should we call down fire from heaven to burn them up?" He rebuked them, saying, "You don't know what manner of spirit you are (Luke 9: 55). Jesus demonstrated He did not come to judge but to *save* the world. His entire earthly walk demonstrated mercy and grace.

In the character of Jesus, we begin to understand mercy from the penalty of the law that He shows us. The same mercy He showed to the woman taken in adultery, whose punishment was death by stoning according to the law of sin and death. He effectively undid the judgment and penalty given to Moses by Himself in Leviticus 20: 10.

Jesus' entire ministry was to demonstrate He had come to fulfill the righteous demands of the Law in His own body. The Jews well understood those penalties listed in Deuteronomy 28. They did NOT understand that because of Jesus, God will not condemn, or invoke penalties and send plagues and diseases on us, which sin brought under the old covenant. **Faith says what God says.**

If you have not read the curse of the law in Deut. 28, do so now. Then write Galatians 3: 13 and speak it over your body daily.

Example prayer:

Sickness is a curse and Jesus has redeemed me from the curses listed in Deuteronomy 28 according to Gal. 3: 13. So I command cursed symptoms to be removed and cast into the sea and they must obey me, according to Mark 11: 23-24. Praise be to the Lord. Amen.

†

Hidden From Your Eyes?

What broke the heart of the Lord? As Jesus approached Jerusalem, He *wept* over it and said, "If you, even you, had only known on this day what would bring you peace--but now it is HIDDEN from your eyes . . . because you did not recognize the day of your visitation (Luke 19: 42).

In Matthew 13: 15, Jesus said people shut their eyes and ears and do not understand with their heart and turn so that He would **"heal them."**

As citizens of the kingdom of Light, we have benefits. Psalm 103: 2-4, says, "Bless the Lord O my soul, and forget none of His benefits; Who pardons all your iniquities, Who **heals** all your diseases; Who redeems your life from the pit, Who crowns you with loving kindness and compassion;"

Benefits that we forget, or do not know we have, are benefits that we most likely do not receive. They are often hidden from our eyes, for two reasons. First, the thief steals benefits from us by blinding our eyes. Second, we do not recognize the day of our visitation. I believe this causes Jesus to weep even today, because He died that we might have life. **Faith says what God says.**

Write your personal prayer verses here and speak

them over your life.

Example prayer:

Father, I ask You to remove whatever is hidden from my eyes and open them to understand the day of my visitation. I rejoice in the truth of what I see by faith in what is not yet seen until it is fully manifest also in my body, soul, and spirit (Prov. 4: 22). Amen.

†

The Healing Message Can Be Divisive

After a pair of women were both instantly healed from such severe scoliosis that they could barely walk, the pastor of that church explained to Evangelist Marty Delmon that he would not be inviting her back again. He could see the two women both walking normally and rejoicing, however he said to Marty, "What you did was just too charismatic for us." She answered, "I'm so sorry I offended you, please forgive me." Marty felt the anointing lift instantly.

Four months later, that pastor was fired.

"Faith in healing is a volatile subject. It can divide churches," says Marty. She adds that a person's experience should not be considered more theologically correct than the Word. "Just because you, or somebody you know, did not experience healing does not make the Word wrong. Failure to receive healing does not change the truth of the Word of God. An illness that is not healed instantly also does not mean sickness is God's will." (Again, I refer readers to Deut. 29:29.)

Can God work an illness for good in someone's life? Certainly. But the illness does not come from God (James 1: 17).

In her own body, Marty has experienced both supernatural and medical healings. Facing a possible hysterectomy, she heard (in her spirit) the Lord asking, "What do you have faith for?" She answered that she could believe for a painless recovery. After the surgery, the nurse offered painkillers, but she never needed even one. Her recovery was painless. God met her at the level of her faith.

How do we pray for others?

Teaching a biblical foundation for healing is so important. Never impose on another what they *should* believe. Supernatural healing can hurt and divide a church membership. However, that is the devil's strategy. I personally wouldn't want to be in a church where prayers for healing do not happen according to James 5: 15. That is the pattern for a believing congregation.

Pray the prayer of faith (take authority over the illness) for the sick *who ask* for prayer. For the sick who do not ask for prayer, pray the Lord will cause the healing word-seed to fall upon their ear and produce faith in their hearts, which will rise up in them to produce the harvest of healing.

When He Persists, Continue To Resist

You can allow Satan the right to continue his attack on your life or you can refuse it. You may have given him the right out of ignorance of the Word (lack of knowledge) or by misconception (religious tradition), **but when you know the truth**, you have every right to resist bondage and oppression, which do not come from God.

When arthritis, cancer, other illnesses have threatened my body in the past, I simply refused it and kept on acting, working, singing, and praising God as though I were completely well. It took a while, but slowly, those symptoms left. Glory to God. That's what James calls *resisting the devil*.

What happens when you don't resist? Nothing good. What happens when you do resist him? James declares, *"He will flee from you!"* (James 4:7). He doesn't always give up easily, but neither do believers who know their rights in Christ. When he persists, they continue to resist. They stand on the promise until victory comes (Eph. 6: 13). **Faith says what God says.**

Write Ephesians 6: 13 and 6: 17 in your prayer journal.

Example prayer:

Father, I resist the devil by speaking with the sword of the spirit, which is the Word of God. I persist in commanding the oppressor to leave my body. I expect to have what I say, instead of saying what I have. Praise God. Healing is mine. Amen!

†

A Lazy Believer?

Do you know what a lazy believer is? One who refuses to seek the Lord. Here's an example. A woman I once knew suffered from severe back pain. She said, "God can heal me any time He wants to." She assumed that because she believed God is *capable* of healing, she was in faith. She left it all up to God and did not bother to seek His kingdom benefits, listed in more than a hundred verses filled with the promise: "I will take sickness away from the midst of you" (Exodus 23: 25). She had never been taught that **faith *takes* what grace provides**.

Consider the woman with the issue of blood. What if she had said, "If Jesus wants to heal me, He will." What if she sat home in accordance with Jewish law (because of her issue of blood) and passively waited for healing to happen? Instead, she did just the opposite. She *heard* about Jesus, *spoke* her faith, *pressed* through the throngs, *touched* His garment, and *took* her healing. **Jesus did not even pray for her or command her illness to depart.** He actually had to ask, "Who touched me?" Trembling, she admitted she was the one.

Jesus did not say, "The *Father* has healed you."

He said, "Daughter, YOUR faith has made you whole," (Luke 8: 48). She is a good example of Matthew 11: 12, "From the days of John the Baptist until now, the kingdom of heaven suffers violence and the violent take it by force." Commentary writers all agree that the violent are eager, full of impetuous zeal to grasp the kingdom's peace, pardon, and blessings with as much eagerness as soldiers carrying off the spoil of a conquered city.

If you do not know how to press in and seize God's promise of healing, continue to meditate on the healing scriptures. Nothing is more powerful than God's word. **Faith says what God says.**

Write Exodus 23: 25 and claim the promise as your own.

Example prayer:

Father, You said You would bless our food and take sickness away from our midst. I thank You for blessing my daily meals, and I claim the promise that sickness is removed from me. Amen.

Faith Says What God Says by Harriett Ford

✝

Faith Takes What Grace Provides

My good friend Wendy Lawson, author of the book, **God's Madcap Missionary**, prayed for a little boy in Africa while she was on a mission trip with Marilyn Hickey. At that time, Wendy did not know how to pray for the sick. The youngster hobbled toward her with so much hope and faith shining in his eyes. Wendy knelt down and grasped his crooked leg. As a nurse, Wendy could see the leg had been broken and never properly set. She prayed a simple prayer: "Father, please heal this little boy's leg."

At once, she felt those misshapen bones begin to move under her hands! The leg became completely normal.

I believe that child's faith pulled healing virtue out of the Lord, just like the woman with the issue of blood pulled healing out of the Lord. I remain amazed that Jesus did not *even pray one word* for her. It was *the woman's faith* that activated the healing, which she received in her body (Luke 8: 43-48).

It seems that faith can reach out and *take* the healing provided in Jesus, even at times *without* any prayer spoken. You can take yours today. **Faith says what God says.**

Write Luke 8: 48 in your prayer journal.

Example prayer:

Father, the woman with the issue of blood believed and her faith made her whole. I am a believer, reaching out to touch my Healer, Jesus. My faith in the power of His word makes me whole. Thank You, Lord. Amen.

†

Do You Want To Be Healed?

Jesus once asked a paralytic, "Do you want to be healed?" (John 5:6). Strangely enough, some people actually do not.

I prayed over woman at a church-benefit sale one morning. She was suffering from back pain. The Lord instantly adjusted her spine and her legs became equal in length. She repeatedly told me throughout the day that her back pain lessened until it was completely gone. Glory to God our healer.

Later, her husband arrived at the church. He was limping and in obvious pain. His wife told him how the Lord had touched her spine and the pain was gone. I asked him if he also wanted prayer. He answered, "No, I'm in pain-training for the Tribulation." He limped throughout the day.

A second fellow, suffering pain from a surgical procedure, refused prayer because the minister did not have what he considered the "proper, holy appearance." What is the proper look anyway?

Both men continued to suffer pain. Wrong believing will rob people of their kingdom benefits (Psalms 103 and 91). Most Christians know that it is not God's will for any to perish. He wants all to come to repentance, (2 Peter 3:9). Sadly, not everyone receives salvation. It is the same with healing. God wants His children to be in health and prosper, (3 John 1: 2). Yet not everyone receives healing and abundant life. Often it is simply due to wrong believing.

Nowhere in the New Testament does God put anyone in pain training. Persecution for the word's sake does not come from God. Why would He persecute His own body? **Faith says what God says.**

Write I Cor. 12: 27 and Rom. 8: 11.

Example Prayer:

Lord, I am a member of the body of Christ according to Your word. I am also a joint heir with Him. He suffered the wrath and penalty for sin in my place and fulfilled all the demands of righteous judgment. I inherit from the Father of spirits, a spirit of love, power, and a sound mind. I do not inherit sickness. Amen.

✝

A Hardened Heart?

"For they did not understand about the loaves, their hearts were hardened. (Mark 6: 52)."

That fellow who believes he must be in pain-training for the tribulation is a god-fearing, church going, Bible-believing man. The Lord shows me that while he believes for salvation, his heart is hardened toward the Lord as our Healer. Even though he knew his wife received instant healing through prayer, he chose to refuse it.

If the disciples of Jesus had hardened hearts in certain areas, so can we. And most of us do.

Many churches get only so far in their understanding and camp there, content with salvation and waiting on the Lord's return. They have been taught wrongly, that the 24 scriptures regarding healing the sick by laying on of hands are no longer in effect today.

Or they have believed a lie that sickness is from God, when clearly it is not. Romans 5:12 states, "Therefore, just as sin came into the world through one man, and death through sin, and so death spread to all men. . ." Sickness is the beginning of death. It comes from the sin of Adam—not from God. Christ came to bring life, to make inoperative the works of the devil, and to reverse the curse of Adam's failure. **Faith says what God says.**

Write First John 3: 8.

Example prayer for family members with hardened hearts:

Father, You said our worst enemies are those under our own roof. Daughters, mothers, sons and in-laws are divided over what they believe about Jesus (Matt. 10: 35). I see that familiarity causes unbelief, just as in Jesus' hometown. Please show me if I have hardened my heart in any place regarding Your works and Your will. I do not know how to overcome hardness of heart in others, except to continue loving them. Please soften the hearts of those who are in need of healing and open their eyes to the truth that sets them free (John 12: 40). Amen.

†

God Spoke Through The TV

Ever notice the methods God sometimes uses to get your attention? I was reading this verse: "The Lord will take away from thee all sickness and will *put none of the evil diseases* of Egypt, which thou knowest, upon thee . . ." (Deut. 7: 15. KJV). I was wondering what those "evil diseases" are, when that very moment, a man on a secular TV program, said, "Evidence of every chronic disease known to modern man has been found in Egyptian mummies."

Wow. That is what I call a get-the-message moment.

Notice God did not say these diseases are good for us, or discipline us, or teach us patience. Did God permit them? Yes. When people stepped out from under the umbrella of obedience, they were subject to the curses in Deuteronomy 28. Aren't you glad we have a new and better covenant?

The Father permits evil in this world because Satan is its ruler and prince (Jn 12: 31; 2 Cor. 4: 3). Disease is not good. It is "evil," and a curse. God always provides a way of escape throughout the Bible. He said He would put none of the evil diseases of Egypt on us and would take away all sickness. So how do we access this blessing? Death and life are in the power of the tongue, and those that love it will eat its fruit (Proverbs 18: 21). Let the redeemed of the Lord say so (Psalm 107: 2).

Write Psalm 107: 2. The enemy is sickness and also any other thing that exalts itself against the knowledge of God (2 Cor. 10: 5). Exalting himself against the knowledge of God is what Satan desires to do. Read the five "I-will" verses of Isa. 14: 13 in which he declares what he wants to do. His will has not changed. Resist it.

Example prayer:

Father, the knowledge of the *law* of the Spirit of life in Christ Jesus is what makes me victorious over the enemy. As I diligently seek knowledge of Your will through the Bible and learn how to operate within the parameters of that law, I overcome the oppressor. Thank You for revealing Jesus, my Healer, as the revelation of Your perfect will. Amen.

†

We Are Flesh Being Made The Word

Knowing the weakness, the ugliness, the failures of my imperfect flesh, I have stumbled at the idea that I could ever become the righteousness of God in Christ. Impossible. I know what my family is thinking about me. But that's okay. God's word is still true. His righteousness is imputed to me, whether I act like it or not!

The verse in Romans 8:29 speaks of believers being conformed to the *image* of Jesus. Also, Psalm 17: 15 speaks of awakening with His *likeness*.

So how does this happen, Lord? I am Your workmanship.

The Lord spoke in In John 1: 14, Jesus is the Word made flesh. Then He whispered to my heart, you are flesh being made the Word.

The more we fill our minds with the Word, the more life we have, and the more we become like our Lord Jesus.

Faith says what God says. John 14: 3 and Heb. 4: 16 here. Speak these verses over your life.

Example prayer:

Father, If I look at my failures and my rebellious ways, I do not have the boldness to approach Your

throne of grace and find mercy. I feel like Isaiah, a man of unclean lips. Then I hear the Holy Spirit's sweet whisper, Do not call unclean what God has called clean. The blood of Jesus makes me clean. I rejoice because in the righteousness of Jesus (not my own) I can come to Your throne of grace, find favor, and be accepted as Your own child. Amen.

†

Little Faith Is Not Unbelief

Maybe a challenge has come against you, and you feel you have little faith. There is a difference between little faith and unbelief.

At times, Jesus said to His disciples, "O you of little faith."

As before mentioned in Mark 9:24, the man who begged Jesus to heal his demon-oppressed child honestly admitted, "Lord I do have faith. Please help me where faith fails." This anguished father had come to Jesus' disciples, and they could not cast out the demon. Note this. When he appealed to Jesus, he called Him LORD. There is respect and *acknowledgement of Jesus as Lord* in the man's words. Even though he admitted having a lack of faith, (a measure of doubt).

Still he had *enough* faith.

Jesus healed his son.

Jesus encountered **unbelief** in His hometown of Nazareth. The home-folks "took offense" at Him and their unbelief stopped Him from performing "mighty works" there (Matt. 13: 55-57).

When the Pharisees saw Him restore a man's withered hand, they conspired to kill Him. That is UNBELIEF. There is no love, no respect in this kind of refusal to believe. **Faith says what God says.**

Read Matt. 12: 10-14. How did the Pharisees

respond? How would you respond?

Example prayer:

Father, at times it seems my faith is weak. But I say I have enough faith to move mountains because *You said* so. I do not doubt that as a joint heir with Jesus, I have a legal right to the healing purchased for me at Calvary with His blood. So, I encourage my faith by looking to Your Word. Thank you for the victory. Amen.

†

You'd Be Foolish Not To

If you were dying and a doctor gave you a prescription, promising that you would completely recover after a number of days, would you take it? You'd be foolish not to.

If God, Who created your body, promised you, "My words are life and health to your whole body, (Prov. 4:22), and if you meditate on them day and night you will completely recover (Josh. 1:8)" would you do it? You'd be foolish not.

Many people never act on these life-giving promises from God, the Creator of the universe. Others, like the woman in the testimony below, took God at His Word.

Testimony:

In the early 1900s, an ambulance brought a woman to the home of retired Dr. Lilian B. Yeomans. Dr. Yeomans knew the patient was in the final stages of tuberculosis. Instead of administering strong drugs, she began to teach scriptures from Deuteronomy 28 and Galatians 3:13. She instructed the woman to repeat to herself every waking moment, **"According to Deuteronomy 28:22, consumption (or tuberculosis) is a curse of the law. But according to Galatians 3:13, Christ has redeemed me from the curse of the law. Therefore, I no longer have tuberculosis."**

For three days, the patient repeated the verses. Near the end of the third day, the woman rushed down the stairs, shouting at the top of her voice, "Sister Yeomans—did you know? Christ has redeemed me, and I no longer have tuberculosis! It's gone now!"

Dr. Yeomans realized that the way into the heart is through renewing the mind with the Truth of God. She knew if the woman would speak often enough, "According to Deuteronomy 28:22, consumption is a curse. But according to Galatians 3:13, Christ has redeemed me from the curse of the law. Therefore, I no longer have tuberculosis," the Word which she continually sowed into her heart for three days, would finally produce a harvest and set her free. -- Source: *Redeemed From Poverty, Sickness, and Spiritual Death* by Kenneth E. Hagin. **Faith says what God says.**

God's word is truth. Write John 8: 31-32 in your prayer journal.

†

God's Good Pleasure

Jesus assured us in Luke 12: 32, "Do not be afraid, little flock, for it is your Father's **good pleasure** to give you the kingdom." That means here on earth as it is in Heaven, (Luke 17:21). That's what we want for our own children. It is our good pleasure to see them in health and prospering even as their souls prosper (3 John: 2).

No father would deliberately put pain and disease on his child. He would go to jail for that.

What person would not do what he could to help even a suffering pet? Yet some people believe God would afflict and scourge His children to "teach them patience," or some other lesson.

God has already done what He could to bring deliverance from sin and sickness to His people. Jesus has already been afflicted and scourged. He gave His authority to believers. It is up to us to resist the thief that tries to steal our freedom from affliction.

Testimony:

Years ago, a doctor diagnosed my little girl with a heart murmur. Another doctor said she showed symptoms of asthma, and still another diagnosed her with scoliosis. When she bent over, I could clearly see one little shoulder blade higher than the other. These physicians said she should not play team sports and would be limited in her life's activities. I simply refused to accept those curses. I didn't even pray about it. I knew those diseases were not from God, and I never mentioned them to her or anyone else. I allowed her to continue her normal activities. She never had a single problem, went on to be a cheerleader in high school, and remains healthy today. Glory to the Lord who watches over His word to perform it. **Faith says what God says.**

Write 3rd John verse 2 and speak it over your life.

A Good Report And An Evil Report

The men sent to spy out the promised land returned with an "evil report" against the land (Numbers 14: 36). Their fearful words described the giants in the land caused the whole camp to fear and disobey God's command.

Only Joshua and Caleb had a different report. They said, "The Lord will bring us into this land and give it to us. We are well able to take the land," (Numbers 13:30).

The evil report is always there, and so also is the good report. Yes, there are giants in the land. However, we are well able to defeat the giants of disease, lack, challenges, addiction, etc. because we know healing and victory IS God's will.

It is up to us to believe the good report in God's word or to deny it and agree with the evil report, however factual it may be. Facts are always subject to change, but God's word is settled forever in heaven.

Exodus 15:26 says He will put none of the evil diseases upon His people which were among the Egyptians. "I will bless your bread and your water and *I will* take sickness away from you," Ex. 23:25. See that? *I will.*

God's word is His will. **Faith says what God says.**

Write Luke 5: 12 and make it your faith confession.

Example prayer:

Father, I thank You that even if I hear an evil report, I am well able to defeat the giant of disease, because you have given me a good report in Your word. I resist fear, doubt, and cast down every word which tries to steal from me what You say is true. I am more than a conqueror through Christ Who strengthens me! Praise God. I am getting up, getting dressed, and going about my daily life in the joy of the Lord. Amen.

Testimony:

Faith is followed by action. I had an attack of vertigo one morning. Extreme nausea and dizziness overwhelmed me. I got out of bed and barely made my way to the restroom where I had to lie down on the floor to keep from falling. I could not lift my head because the room kept spinning round me.

I said, "Father, You are my Healer. What should I do?" I heard His voice asking, "What would you be doing normally?" Normally, I would walk on the treadmill at this time. I knew He was telling me that if I truly believed in I Peter 2:24, **I would act like it.** So, I got up and held onto the walls to keep from falling.

The wave of dizziness and nausea continued, but I made my way upstairs and got on the treadmill. I had to hold the handle bars and felt like I would vomit at any moment, but I kept walking. Within ten minutes of acting like I was healed, all nausea and dizziness completely disappeared. It has never returned.

Faith says what God says. Write James 2: 14-17. Describe how you plan to act like the promise you are believing to receive is true, even though it is not yet manifest.

†

Daughter Of Abraham

Jesus said, "Ought not this woman, a daughter of Abraham whom Satan has bound for 18 years **be loosed from this** bond on the Sabbath day?" (Luke 13:17).

Ought not Your daughters, Lord, be loosed also, according to Galatians 3:29, which says we who believe in **Christ are Abraham's seed** and heirs of God? Yes! Healing is the children's bread, (Mark 7: 27) according to Jesus.

We are joint heirs with the Lord Jesus. We do not inherit sickness from anyone but Adam and because we are new creations born again into the family of God, we are no longer subject to the law of sin and death (Rom.8: 2). **Faith says what God says.**

Write Romans 8: 2 and 8: 17 here and speak these verses over your life.

Example prayer:

Father, Your word declares I am a daughter (son) of Abraham and a joint heir with Jesus my Lord. I take up my weapons of spiritual warfare, which are Your mighty Words—the sword of the Spirit. I speak to the enemy of my flesh. Get thee behind me Satan! I declare I am loosed from Satan's bondage.

†

Praise God. Drowning Is Not An Option

When you hold a sleeping baby in your arms, are you not amazed at how trustfully he sleeps? Remember when Jesus was sleeping in the boat on raging seas, and the terrified disciples woke Him to say, "Don't You care that we're about to sink?"

Jesus had already spoken these words, "Let us go over to the other side." He went to sleep, confident that what He speaks always comes to pass.

I believe He was resting in the Father's arms, peacefully sleeping like a trusting child, never doubting He would arrive safely, no matter how strong the tempest.

Of course, He did rebuke the wind and waves when they woke Him.

You can do the same.

Example prayer:

Father, I speak to the storm of medical reports. Peace be still. You rescued everyone on the boat with Jesus and also everyone on the ship with Paul when the storms threatened. I thank You that no matter how strong the storm (the challenge) in my life, I am going over to victory on the other side. Praise God who calms the wind and waves and watches over His word to perform it. I will rest in His peace that

passes understanding. Amen.

Drowning is not an option when Jesus is in the boat.
The Prayer of Agreement (Matt. 18: 19)

In My name, there am I with them." (Matt. 18:19-20). When Jesus says **Truly**, He means *truly*. I used to think the meaning of this verse is that we simply both agree that we want healing and ask for healing in prayer. Not exactly, because everyone agrees they want the sick to be healed.

What this teaching really means is that we agree together that God's word is true (has authority over the doctor's report, no matter how factual the medical condition is) and we know that as we continue to stand in agreement on His Word, Jesus is there with us to see that the Word is performed.

Example prayer:

Father, we honor Your Word today and agree together with believers of like precious faith (not doubt) that Your word is settled forever. By Jesus' stripes we are healed. Thank you, Jesus, for what you said to us "truly." I receive it truly. Amen.

†

Salvation Is Threefold

We are created a tribune being in the image of the trinity. God is Father, Son, and Holy Spirit. So, what three parts are we? We are body, soul, and spirit, (I Thess. 5: 23).

Hebrews 4: 12 states that only the Word of God can "divide asunder soul and spirit, and of the joints and marrow." I cannot define the difference adequately.

Here's what is important. Salvation happens for all three parts of us. Not just our spirits, as I wrongly understood for many years. Simply put, our spirit is saved at the new birth (John 3: 5-6). Our soul is being saved by the renewing of the mind (Eph. 4: 22-32) and our body will be saved at the resurrection when what is corruptible shall put on incorruptible (I Cor. 15: 54).

When Jesus sweat drops of blood, He was taking on all the sorrows and griefs (our soul wounds) of the whole human race (Isa. 53: 4). He was pierced for our transgressions (our spiritual death), and by His stripes we were healed (physical illness). If you question that physical illness is part of the package, look at Matthew 8: 17, which clearly states Jesus healed physical bodies to fulfill Isaiah's prophecy. He is still healing diseases today because He is the same, yesterday, today, and forever.

He paid the penalty for all three parts of our triune being. That does not mean that we don't have soul wounds or physical illnesses, or that our bodies will not die. That means the curse of the Law has been fulfilled. Our appointment with physical death does not change because of Adam's curse. However, our spirits have already passed from death to eternal life! (John 5: 24). Our bodies have been redeemed from the curse of all sickness and disease listed in Deuteronomy 28: 15-68. We need only to receive by faith what Jesus provided (Galatians 3: 13). Sorrow comes, but we sorrow not as the world sorrows (I Thess. 4: 13). Soul wounds and illnesses will happen, but as we renew our minds (souls) we learn to overcome by the blood of the Lamb and the word of our testimony. **Faith says what God says.**

Write Eph. 4: 23-24 in your prayer journal.

†

Armies In Heaven?

Have you ever wondered why God needs armies in heaven?

My meditation this morning was on Revelation 12, how the devil and his angels made war in heaven. WAR in Heaven?!

War is such an ugly word. What a completely incongruous thought. Totally opposite of what we usually think Heaven is about.

War began in heaven when the devil and his angels were kicked out and then set up the kingdom of darkness on the earth. The war isn't quite over yet, although the outcome is finished, according to the Lord.

When Jesus taught us to pray, "Thy kingdom come, Thy will be done on earth as it is in heaven," that prayer takes on multiple meanings. One meaning is that we are praying for the heavenly kingdom to come back to the earth when Jesus returns as King of kings and Lord of Lords. There is yet a second meaning, but I will speak of it later.

A third meaning is that we should **kick the devil's works out of our lives here on earth just as he was kicked out of heaven. And that "your days may be multiplied and the days of your children . . . as the days of heaven on earth"** (Deut. 11: 21).

We cannot turn off the darkness, but we can

overcome it with the Light of the World. **Faith says what God says.**

Write Rev. 12: 11. What is the word of your testimony?

†

Where Is Satan's Realm?

Popular thought usually assumes Satan resides in Hell. This could not be farther from the truth, although Hell is his final destination after the thousand-year reign (Rev. 20: 10). I remember my astonishment at discovering that Jesus called him the prince of the power of the air and also the ruler of this present world (Eph. 2: 2).

Where is the "power of the air"? Theologians and Bible scholars agree it is the atmosphere, the heavenly realms around the earth, which is the first of three heavens (2 Cor. 12: 2).

Ephesians 6: 12 speaks of believers whose "struggle is not against flesh and blood, but against the rulers, against the authorities, against the powers of this dark world and against the spiritual forces of evil in the **heavenly realms**."

These rulers, authorities, and powers are not flesh and blood. They are spirits under the rule of Satan, who made war in heaven. They were cast out with a third of his angels. (Rev. 12: 7-12). Satan uses them to work his evil designs in the earth, just as the Father works through His people to establish His kingdom on earth.

Satan spoke through Peter. He entered Judas. He sometimes speaks to us through our own family members (Luke 12: 53). How do we handle this? Just like Jesus did. "Get thee behind me Satan. **It is written.**

. ." Faith says what God says.

Write I Peter 5: 8 and Matt. 16: 18-19 below. What written words do you speak to combat roaring lies?

Example Prayer:

It is written, get behind me Satan. God has imputed the righteousness of Jesus to me. Therefore, you have no authority over me or my household. I bind the evil spirits attacking me or my family and command them to leave in the name of Jesus. I loose the power of the Holy Spirit to drive them out. I rejoice in the goodness of God, my Savior. Amen.

†

Deliver Us From The Evil One (Matt. 6:13)

Jesus taught us to ask for our daily bread. DAILY bread. We know that it is the Father's will to give us food (Matt. 6: 8). Yet Jesus teaches us to ask for it *daily*. Why? We are increasing our trust and glorifying God when we acknowledge Him in all our ways rather than taking our daily bread for granted.

Healing is also clearly the children's **bread** spoken of in Matthew 15. So, it is right to praise Him for our daily healing as well.

The next part of the Lord's prayer deals with temptation. To be sick is actually a temptation when we understand that sickness is part of the kingdom of darkness—the natural world in which we live. This world is under the curse and is presently ruled by the Prince of the kingdom of darkness.

We are NOT part of that kingdom when we have been born again. (Col. 1:13). That is why we are to pray the Father will deliver us from the evil one daily. Many translations say only, "deliver us from evil," however the older manuscripts include the word "one." Evil is always credited to Satan. **Faith says what God says.**

Write Matt. 6: 8.

†

God Is All About Love?

The Lord is not slack concerning his promise, as some men count slackness; but is long-suffering to us-ward, not willing that any should perish, but that all should come to repentance (2 Peter 3: 9).

I have a friend who says God is all about love, and all people are embraced by Him even if they choose to ignore His warning against dangerous lifestyles.

Suppose your daughter and son were going to a celebration at a nearby lake. You gave them a warning.

"Enjoy all the fun, kids, but stay out of the water. It's contaminated with a deadly virus."

Suppose they arrived and saw people in the water. One of the swimmers said, "Come on in. The water's fine."

They decided their dad didn't really know what he was talking about, and they also went into the water. Later they were admitted to the hospital where they saw the same swimmers in critical condition. Their recovery was uncertain.

You didn't want that to happen because you love your children so much. They chose to ignore your word and reaped painful consequences.

God is the same. The reason He hates sin so much is because it separates us from Him. He wants to have an intimate relationship with each of us. When we ignore

His warning, we disrespect His word. We decide for ourselves what is right and wrong. That hurts the Father of spirits because He knows it will eventually destroy us.

He made a way of escape for disobedient children, but if they continue to ignore His Word, he cannot help them.

Make no mistake. Sin does not go unpunished. Thankfully, there is a remedy in Jesus, but without Him, there is only destruction. Eternal destruction (2 Pet. 3: 9).

✝

Testimony

If Satan cannot kill you with disease, he will resort to lies. An evil spirit manifested itself to Evangelist Tim Thompson one night. It appeared as the virgin Mary (2 Cor. 11: 14) and began to speak to him, saying, "I know how you have struggled. I know how tired you are. The Lord says you can come home now." The spirit enticed him to take his own life and promised to hold him lovingly him until he died.

Tim immediately recognized the spirit, whose actual name is Suicide. He commanded it to leave in Jesus' Name. The spirit left him.

As a former psychic and Satanic priest, Tim has denounced all ties with the demonic spirit world. He is now a highly respected minister of deliverance, reaching out to people who have been ensnared in witchcraft, Satanism, and the occult world. **Healing Is The Children's Bread.**

I used to think that if I did not see an answer to prayer at once, then it must not be God's will. I was wrong. Notice how the Lord ministered to the Canaanite woman. He first ignored her. Then He actually called her a dog.

When she came to Jesus asking Him to heal her daughter, He answered, "It is not right to take the children's bread and toss it to the dogs."

Clearly, He was speaking of healing. She asked Him

for healing. He said healing is "the children's bread." The "children" are the elect, the Jewish children of Abraham, Isaac, and Jacob. And the Canaanite woman was *not* a Jew.

In Matt. 15:24, the Lord said, "I was sent ONLY to the lost sheep of the house of Israel." His ministry was to the Jew first. However, He also ministered to Gentiles who believed in Him. They drew healing out of Him by their words of faith.

The Lord knew this woman had faith in her heart, and He coaxed it out of her—got her to speak faith words—so that He had a legal right to heal her daughter even *before* His resurrection when the temple veil was opened to Gentiles also. When she said "the dogs eat the crumbs under their *master's* table," she was acknowledging Jesus as Master. That is faith in the Messiah, not unbelief. Also, she humbly did not suggest she was worthy in herself. Self-righteousness never wins a blessing.

Example prayer:

Father, You sent Jesus, the living bread down from heaven. He said there is no death (of the spirit) for those who eat His flesh and drink His blood. He was not talking about eating literal flesh and blood (John 6: 63) but about the covenant meal foreshadowed by the perfect Passover lamb in Egypt. That blood provided healing to a million Hebrews (Psa. 105: 37). By saying this, Jesus proclaimed Himself the New-Covenant-sacrificial

Lamb (John 6: 50-52). I enter into the blood covenant and I receive the children's bread (healing) as a joint heir with Jesus. Amen.

†

What Are Your Eyes Fixed On?

"So, we fix our eyes not on what is seen, but on what is not seen," (2 Cor. 4: 18).Faith is the evidence of things that are not seen. We **look NOT** to the things that are **seen (doctor's and lab reports, which are subject to change)** but to the things that are **Unseen**. For the things that are **seen** are transient, temporary. They will pass away. The things that are **unseen** are eternal. **Faith says what God says.**

Write Psalm 16: 8 and 2 Cor. 5: 7. Declare that you will not be moved from your stand on the healing words which are written.

Example prayer:

Lord, I am fixing my eyes on Your healing promises. I am renewing my imagination and my faith by looking to the eternal Truth in I Peter 2:24, which is settled forever in Heaven. I am calling the supernatural healing by the stripes of Jesus out of the *unseen* world and into the natural world. I am imitating my Father God Who called those things that were not seen as though they were (Rom 4:17). I'm resisting doubt and calling up faith from inside my spirit, to stand on the solid Rock until my healing is complete. Amen! Praise God.

†

Imagine Yourself Well

My understanding needs to be renewed every day. My well needs to be kept free of debris which stop the flow of living water.

Proverbs 3: 6-8 speaks of trusting in the Lord rather than your own understanding (which medically trained people tend to do, and so do most of us who are walking only by natural sunlight (instead of supernatural SON light). Keeping God's word before your eyes shall be "health to your navel and marrow to your bones," according to Proverbs 3: 6-8.

I continually renew my understanding according to God's word and visualize my immune system producing good health. Whatever I can imagine, I can have, according to Genesis 11: 6. Isn't that good news!? **Faith says what God says.**

Write Gen. 11: 6 and 2 Cor. 10: 5.

Example prayer:

Lord Jesus, I see the Father called those things into existence which were not yet in the physical realm in Romans 4:17. I renew my imagination, seeing health instead of illness. I continue to speak life to my body, bone marrow, organs, eyes, ears, and I say, blood, marrow, joints, immune system,

organs, I command you to be normal. You have to obey me, according to Mark 11: 23-24. Praise Jesus, I am healed by faith, not by feelings. Amen.

The above prayer is how I combat arthritis which has tried to manifest in my feet and hands. It is gone!! Hallelujah.

†

I Am The Healed

In Exodus 15: 26, God declares, "I am Jehovah-Rapha the God Who heals you."

Every time I say the words, I AM, I'm speaking His name. Today I will add, "I am the healed," each time I speak His Name. I will declare it aloud also, because Mark 11: 23-24 says I must speak what I believe *before* I shall have what I say. The Lord spoke things into existence in the same manner. Abraham imitated God, Who called those things which were not yet in existence as though they were (Rom. 4: 17). So also did Jonah, David, Hannah, the Shunamite woman, and every prophet in the Bible.

In Isaiah 53: 5, God called Jesus the One who *heals* us by His stripes. This declaration was made hundreds of years before Jesus was born into the earth. By God's declaration, we were saved and healed before we were even born.

Write Ephesians 1: 4 here.

†

Do Not Limit God

I have said this before. It is worth repeating. We parents love to bless our children and would do anything in our power for them. However, we are limited in what we can do.

God is the same. He loves to bless His children. He gave us His Son on the cross to purchase us from the kingdom of darkness and translate us into the Kingdom of Light. That makes you and I valuable beyond compare.

Do you realize that God is also limited? He is limited by unbelief. People perish through ignorance of His word, Hosea 4:6.

Lack of knowledge of His Word, His will, or wrong believing can take a while to overcome, but it can certainly be defeated. You have the victory when you renew Your mind according to His word. Knowledge of the Word is a key to the kingdom. Once you know it, you release faith by speaking it. His Word does not return to Him empty. Praise God. **Faith says what God says.**

Write the first line in Hosea 4: 6 and declare you will not die from lack of knowledge.

†

Encourage Myself In The Lord

"I waited for the Lord on high, and He heard my cry. He brought me up out of the pit of destruction, out of the miry clay. He set my feet upon a rock and made my footsteps firm, "(Psalm 40: 1-3).

When I look at some circumstances of the miry clay in the world, it is easy to become discouraged. So, I refuse to look at them. Instead, I will encourage myself in my Lord as King David did in I Sam. 30: 6. In almost every Psalm, when David began with a plea for help, he ended with a note of victory, believing that God heard his cry even *before any circumstance changed*. That is faith, speaking and acting on the evidence of things not seen.

King David declared the answer *before it came to be*. That is perfectly in line with Romans 4:17, how God calls things that are not (not yet evident in the physical world) as though they were. In Psalm 28, David begins by calling out, "Help Lord." He describes a serious problem for a few verses. By verse six, he is declaring the answer, praising God because, He has "heard my cry for help."

Does anyone think the help arrived before David even finished writing five verses? No. David was declaring by faith, those things that be not as though they were.

When the enemy attacks my body with a curse of

sickness, I declare what God said. Let the redeemed of the Lord say so. I am redeemed from the curse of sickness (Gal. 3: 13). He sent His word and healed me, (Psalm 107: 20). The Lord has healed me and I am healed. People may think I'm crazy, or even lying, when the symptoms are still obvious, but God's word is still true. I have His word (I Pet. 2:24) that by His stripes I was healed, not will be healed. I have it now, regardless of whether I look like it. As I fight the good fight of faith, the Lord makes me victorious. Praise God, I am healed. **Faith says what God says.**

Write Psalm 18: 2-3 and declare it is true.

Example prayer:

Father God, You are greater than any enemy we may face. I thank You for delivering me from the enemy's attempt to send me to the pit of destruction. Instead of miry clay, my feet are planted on the solid Rock, which is Jesus. I shall not be moved. Praise God. Amen.

†

Striving Or Resting?

It is always good to continue praying and ask people of faith to pray also, yet because of deep concern, I find it's easy to fall into striving to exercise faith rather than to *rest* in it.

Throughout the ordeal of my husband's on-going treatment for cancer, I rested in faith, for the most part, riding on wings of prayer from others. Then concern would rise up, and I would claim again and again God's healing touch. The Lord gave me a gentle rebuke.

Lord, you have already heard my petition. I have argued my case in the court of heaven. So how do I pray when concern (fear, doubt) rises up?

He seemed to whisper, just praise Me for the answer.

Rest is always the by-product of abiding faith. Am I striving for faith or resting in faith today? The absence or the presence of peace will answer this question. **God inhabits the praises of His people.**

Write Isa. 26:3 and Psalm 63: 3 here and speak praises to God.

Cursed Is The Ground

People point to the toxic and polluted world we live in and blame this for many of the diseases suffered by mankind. That is actually quite true.

"Cursed is the ground because of you (Adam); through painful toil you will eat food from it all the days of your life. It will produce thorns and thistles for you, and you will eat the plants of the field," (Genesis 3: 17-19).

What? We have been eating food grown in cursed ground!? The Old Testament saints lived hundreds of years before their bodies succumbed to death. It took a while for the perfection of the world to become toxic. But it happened. Death and disease entered the world through sin (Rom. 5: 12-13).

My Lord always blessed the bread and water before eating. Why? He was *reversing the curse* brought on the soil. He has redeemed His people from the curse by tasting death for every man, according to Heb. 2: 9. **Faith says what God says.**

Write John 6: 51 and 6: 63. Which of these verses speak of profiting the believer? Christ's *words* or His flesh?

Example prayer:

Father, I put You in remembrance of Your word which says You shall bless my bread and water; and You will take sickness away from me, (Exodus 23-26). Today I eat blessed natural food. And I also eat blessed spiritual food which is the Bread of Heaven and the living Word (I John 1:1). I receive life from the Word for my spirit, soul, and body according to Proverbs 4: 20-22. Thank You Jesus. Amen.

†

Do You Have Ought Against Any?

Forgive, that your Father in heaven may forgive you (Mark 11: 25-26).

If I have suffered wrong, vengeance is in God's hands. Not mine. He asks His people to forgive. Even it is a serious crime? Yes. Forgiving a crime does not mean to excuse it. Crimes and evil do not go unpunished. I trust the Lord to deal with every act of evil.

When we forgive wrongs, we reap benefits that might otherwise be lost. James instructs us to confess our sins to one another that we may be **healed** (James 5: 16). I believe this also means to ask forgiveness of others we may have offended or wronged. Healing is part of the package.

Have I examined my heart and asked the Lord to show me any wicked way? Have I forgiven every offense, no matter how wronged I have been over the years?

I choose to imitate Jesus, who said "Father, forgive them," even as He hung on the cross, for if I do not forgive, how shall I be forgiven?

Example prayer:

Father, I repent of all unforgiveness in my heart. I choose to forgive every person who has ever

wounded me, even though they may not even ask this of me. Create in me a clean heart as David prayed in Psalm 51: 10. Now I speak to my own heart, *Be of good courage.* My hope is in the Lord and in His every promise in the atonement. Thank you, Lord, for cleansing and strengthening my heart today.

†

The God Of Abundant Supply

There is no shortage in God's Storehouse.

Imagine how Peter's wife might have felt when he said, "Honey, I'm leaving to follow a man I believe is the Messiah. "What? You're leaving home to follow a man you hardly know? How long will you be gone? What are we supposed to do for food while you're gone?" He hands her a sack filled with coins and says: "This money is from a single catch! We fished all night and caught nothing. Then Jesus told us to cast our nets on the other side. My nets were almost bursting. I sold them in the marketplace, and there is enough money here to last you until I return."Our God is the God of abundant supply. It would be uncharacteristic of Jesus to ask a man to leave his family without providing for them. He provides everything we need before we even ask (Luke 12: 22-34). **Faith says what God says.**

Write Matt. 6: 26 and 2 Peter 1: 3. Speak these verses back to God.

Testimony:

"Oh Lord, am I selfish to want a healing when there are so many who are very sick and some of them so young?" Police Captain LV of Houston asked God this question when he attended a meeting where healings were happening. In his spirit, he heard the words, "There is no shortage in My storehouse." Captain LV received instant healing from advanced cancer that day. A month later, he told his surgeon he was healed. The doctor all but called him crazy. "The only thing keeping you alive is medication!" The captain smiled and said, "I haven't taken it for about a month." A thorough exam and X-rays showed no cancer. Even his varicose veins had been healed! There is no shortage in God's storehouse.

Does God Care About Pets?

Below is a request from a friend who asked prayer for her beloved kitty

"Harriett, the veterinarian finally called and said Cleopatra (my kitty) did well with anesthesia and the surgery. But part of the tissue he removed with the tumor looked suspicious for cancer so he sent it to pathology. Will have to wait for that report. She can come home tomorrow and will be on antibiotics and pain meds.

I would like to request that You pray for my Cleopatra, because I'm sure God would hear you better than Me, cause I ain't near as good a person as You are.

I'm really stressed. This is the kitty I raised from about a week old, her mom and siblings got killed by a dog. The lady that had her said she figured the only way she would survive was to bring it to me. She is nine years old now. Fed her with a syringe because she didn't know how to suck on a bottle. I was up night and day with her for nearly two months.

She is a very long story and is very special to me. I'll send You a picture of her.

Thank you for caring and please pray for my baby. I Love you, Llewellyn"

I replied: My sweet friend, Llewellyn, God doesn't hear my prayers any better than He hears yours. It's not our goodness or our own righteousness that qualifies us for His blessings. It's the Lord Jesus, who imputes to us His own righteousness. So, we can stand boldly at the throne of grace as joint heirs with the Son of God, and the Father hears our prayers.

Of course, I'm praying for Cleopatra's recovery, and I believe she shall get well, because of Mark 11:23-24. Look up that verse and speak it out loud. Say this:

"Lord, in the name of Jesus I speak to that illness and command it to be removed and cast into the sea. I declare my kitty shall recover and, according to Your word, I shall have what I say.

"I thank You, Jesus, that I have a healthy cat. Amen."

I do not doubt it. She will live out her full life span. Now I wait for good news. You relax. Get a good night's rest. All is well.

Good news. The vet called to say Cleopatra does not have cancer. She will live!

†

Did Jesus Ever Suffer An illness?

Was Jesus Ever Sick? An interesting question.

All of us have lost a loved one or church member while praying with all the faith we had. What does this mean?

God has secrets and mysteries, but the things that are revealed belong to us and to our children, (Deut. 29:29). Jesus revealed the perfect will of God when He went about destroying the works of the devil (Acts 10: 38) healing all that were sick.

Let's think about this "sharing in the suffering of Christ" thing. I have heard it taught that illness is part of that.

I asked the Lord if He ever suffered an illness before He went to the cross. No! He never did. He lived as a Jewish Rabbi under the law of Moses, and He kept it perfectly. Illness is a curse under the law in Deuteronomy 28: 15-28. Jesus said Satan could find "no place" in Him (John 14: 30).

Can Satan bring the curse of disease on a righteous man? What about Job? Yes, but Satan had to get permission first.

What does that say about me, living so far beneath the perfect standard of righteousness that Jesus has set before us?

Good news. He has suffered the curse for us already, (Gal. 3: 13) and He has imputed His righteousness to us

(II Cor. 5: 21).

This is too wonderful to absorb at once. It takes meditation and revelation. It takes receiving. All praises and thanksgiving to God! But then, what suffering of Christ do we share? He made it clear that both tribulation and persecution are "because of the word's sake." (Matt. 13: 20-21).

The only suffering Christ went through was persecution because He preached the Word of God. Because He IS the Word of God! He said all who live godly in Him will suffer persecution. Why? God has an enemy. But be of good cheer. Christ has overcome the world.

Jesus Knew The Pain Of Losing A Loved One

Another curious question. Why? Because he has the power of resurrection. Very likely Mary's husband Joseph died before Jesus began His public ministry. The gospels make no mention of him after he moved the family from Egypt to Nazareth. He is not mentioned as coming with Mary and Jesus' sisters and brothers when they went to summon Him from a house where He was teaching. Joseph was not at the crucifixion. We know that Jesus assigned the care of Mary to the apostle John, so she was apparently widowed at that time.

So, when Joseph died, Jesus did not raise him from the dead. Did Mary blame Him for that, like the sister of Lazarus who said "If you had been here, my brother would not have died."

What is apparent is that it is appointed to all of us once to die and after that the judgment. It is also apparent that Jesus was acquainted with sorrow for the loss of a loved one. He did not rescue his cousin John the Baptist from prison. Could that have happened if He so chose? The man who stopped the wind and waves, who walked on water, and fed 5,000 and then again 4,000. The man who raised the dead. Why did He not stop John's execution? Clearly, Jesus does not force His will on anyone, including those who persecute Him and His followers.

†

Can We Blame God For The Evil In The world?

No. God gave man dominion. It is up to His people to take a stand against the darkness (Luke 10: 19). This is a profound statement in its very simplicity. We must learn how to operate in His authority.

"Depart from Me."Miracle Workers Who Work Iniquity This passage in Matthew 7: 21-23 used to scare me. How could anyone who did miracles in the name of the Lord be lost?

The Hebrew word "yada" means to share love that bears fruit. It is first found in Genesis regarding Adam and his wife Eve.

So, when Jesus told those who claimed they worked miracles and cast out demons in His name, "I never knew (yada) you, ye workers of iniquity,"

He was saying that he never saw them bear the fruit of sharing intimacy with Him. I'm checking my fruit. The Holy Spirit makes it even more clear when we look at Judas. He was one of the twelve who went out to perform miracles in Jesus' name according to Luke 9:2.

The apostles were given power and authority over all demons, to heal the sick and proclaim the kingdom of God. Judas did this. Yet he was a thief who stole from the money bag (John 12: 6).

No one would deny that stealing from Jesus is a work of iniquity. And no one would deny that betraying our Lord is a work of iniquity. Surely to walk with the Lord and yet continue in stealing and greed to satisfy oneself is to be in the category *of never bearing the fruit of sharing intimacy* with Jesus.

Father, deliver from the evil one. Spirit of truth help us to recognize his lies. Amen

†

We Are Not Born Perfect

I hear it almost every day. We are all God's children. It's true that we are all His creation, and He loves each of us enough to die for. But only those who receive Him as Lord can become the true children of God.

"But as many as *received* him, to them gave He *power* to become the sons of God, even to them that believe on His name: Which were born, not of blood, nor of the will of the flesh, nor of the will of man, but of God. (John 1:12-13 KJV)."

We are not born perfect. **We are born as spiritual children of the devil,** according to John 8: 44. That's why we must be born again and why we must never marry an unbeliever. We don't want the devil as our father-in-law!

Ephesians 2: 3 also establishes this, saying that we are all "*by nature* children of wrath." God is the Father of spirits, (Heb. 12:9). Our spirits must be reborn, which means to be united as one with the Spirit of Christ (2 Cor. 5:17). According to I John 3:9, the incorruptible seed of God makes the re-born spirit incapable of sin. "We know that **no one who is born of God (in the newly created spirit)** sins; but He who was born of God keeps himself and the evil one does not touch him."

Wait a minute. Doesn't John also say that if we claim to have no sin, the truth is not in us? Yes he does. *The flesh is still very much capable of sinning.* As Paul says in Romans 7:18, ". . .in my flesh dwells no good thing." The flesh is not the same as our reborn spirit. That's why we need to renew our minds daily.

Faith says what God says. Write John 8: 44 and 2 Cor. 5: 17. If you have any doubt that your spirit has been reborn, read Romans 10: 8-10. Note the emphasis on the spoken words.

†

Can A Demand Be Presumption?

In the Kingdom of Light, a sick person does not make a **demand** on the Father to heal his body. If he has renewed his mind to God's word, he doesn't have to beg God to change His mind and restore health. What good would that do if sickness truly was the will of God?

Instead the believer makes a demand on *the enemy* not to steal, kill or destroy the good works which Jesus has appointed for him to do (Eph. 2: 10). That is a huge difference.

Yes, we rejoice that our names are written in the Lamb's Book of Life, and the greatest miracle is salvation, however countless lives have been blessed by believers who could have chosen to go home before their time and be with Jesus like Paul desired to do: "I have a desire to depart and to be with Christ, which is far better, but it is more important for me to stay in this world for your sake," (Philippians 1: 23-24). Paul chose to remain for the benefit of the believers.

Faith says what God says. Write John 10: 10 and Ephesians 2: 10 and declare to the enemy that he cannot steal from you.

Example prayer:

I demand the oppressor to leave my body in the

Name of Jesus. I am God's workmanship, created in Christ Jesus to do good works, according to Ephesians 2:10. I refuse to let the enemy steal God's plan for my life. I thank You, Lord, for restoring my strength and renewing my youth like the eagle (Isa. 40: 31 and Psalm 25: 2). I rejoice that my name is written in the Lamb's Book of Life. Amen.

†

The Prayer Of Agreement

People of faith have learned much about confessing the word of God. Saying what God says. Speaking to the mountain (the illness or challenge) and commanding it to be cast into the sea—instead of begging God to do something about it. What I feel the Lord has spoken to my heart is this:

I can speak to my mountain and stand in faith until it disappears. I cannot speak to another person's mountain, unless I have their full agreement. My realm of authority is limited. I'm not saying anyone should deny the physical reality of a disease. I'm saying that if you and I continue to agree with what the enemy is trying to put on you, perhaps we have not yet learned how to agree with the truth that sets us free (Matt. 18: 19). That truth is the seed (the word-seed in I Pet. 2: 24) which the enemy is trying to steal from you.

Words will work against you or for you. I can speak to your mountain, but without your agreement, it will probably remain.

For example, a person continually says, "I have cancer. The treatment makes me sick, and I'm not getting any better. the tumor is not responding. The doctor says I'm going to die." That's agreement with negative facts. Walking in the natural realm only.

The believer who walks by faith and not by sight is saying, "I have been diagnosed with cancer, however the Word of the Lord says cancer is a curse. Jesus has redeemed me from the curse. I am healed by His stripes. I receive my healing by faith. I will stand in faith no matter what the disease or the doctors are saying. I have commanded the cancer to be removed and it has to go. I will fight this disease both in the natural and in the supernatural realm. Please agree with me that the Word of God has greater power, and the cancer has to bow its knee to the Name of Jesus."

Matthew 18: 19 says that if two agree on earth as touching anything, it will be done. Do not be double minded. Dig in and having done all to stand, stand therefore. You are appointed to victory. **Faith says what God says.**

Write what stands out most to you from Ephesians 6: 13-18.

†

Neither Do I Condemn You

Jesus bent down and wrote on the dusty stones of the Temple courtyard while the self-righteous Jews waited for Him to stone the woman taken in the act of adultery (John 8:7-8). What He wrote that day, no one knows.

His was the finger that wrote on stone tablets, "Thou shalt not commit adultery" (Ex. 31: 18). His was the finger that wrote, "weighed in the balances and found wanting" (Dan. 5: 27). His was the finger that wrote the *death penalty* for adultery under Old Testament law (Lev. 20: 10).

The very finger of God, Who wrote the law, stood there, knowing He was soon to pay the death penalty required by that law. He was ready to fulfill the righteous demands of the law so that the adulterous woman would not have to die.

"Neither do I condemn you. Go and sin no more."

With every encounter described in the gospels, Jesus demonstrated that He came *not* to condemn the world but to save it. I believe the accusers probably brought that woman stripped naked to the Lord. I seemed to see Him in my mind, wrapping her in His mantel. What a beautiful picture of mercy covering sin. With every healing, He demonstrated that He came to redeem us from the curse of the law of sin and death. What an unspeakable gift the Father has given to us, wrapped by Mary on the first Christmas day. Rejoice! **Faith says**

what God says.

Write John 12: 47 and praise God for its meaning in your life.

†

It Was Satan Who Bound Her

Consider the woman in Luke 13: 16 who suffered 18 long years stooped over, unable to stand straight. Was this God's will? We know she was a daughter of Abraham, and therefore subject to the law of Moses. The Jews would have judged her guilty of some violation of the law, since she was living under the curse described in Deuteronomy 28:15-68.

Did she sin? Of course. None living can say they are not guilty of sin. (Psalm 51:5; 1 John 1:8). Did her violation provoke God *so that He bound her* into a stooped position? No. In Jesus' own words, it **was *Satan who bound her*.** Not God. That is a revelation of where the curses come from. And also a revelation of God's will.

Jesus said, "Should not this woman whom **Satan has kept bound be set free**."

The Lord spoke to my heart. It was *always* God's will that she be set free from that condition. Otherwise Jesus would have been going against the Father's will, and a house divided will not stand. Jesus said, "Truly, truly I say to you, the Son can do nothing by himself; He can do only what He sees the Father doing (John 5:19-20)."

God loosed her from Satan's grip. Why did God wait 18 years to loose her? We will consider that question on the next page.

Have you suffered for years with a chronic illness? Has someone convinced you it is God's will? Think again. Jesus wants you set free just as much as He wanted the stooped woman to be free.

Why Did She Suffer So Long? When I asked that question about the stooped woman described in Luke 13: 10-17, I honestly did not know the answer as to why she waited 18 years for healing. Then I saw that Jesus gave that stooped woman a *privileged* identity when He called her a daughter of Abraham. She had covenant rights to healing.

God expects His people to look to Him for healing. In the thirty-ninth year of his reign King Asa was afflicted with a disease in his feet. "Though his disease was severe, even in his illness he did not seek help from the LORD, but only from the physicians. . ." (2 Chron. 16: 12).

Asa did not seek healing from the Lord. The implication is that he should have done so. Please note, God heals through physicians every day. They are an important part of His healing delivery system in the natural. Never ignore sound medical advice.

The stooped woman had recourse, as a Jew, to **look** at the scriptures in Numbers 21: 4-9 and 2 kings 18: 4 and **see how** the bronze serpent was lifted up on a wooden staff for **healing**. When the bronze serpent was lifted up, the people who **LOOKED at it, did not die** from the deadly venomous snake bite. They recovered.

Satan kept this woman stooped so she could not **look** anyone in the eye. The enemy did not want her to **look** upon Jesus, the One Who just days later, would be lifted up, like the bronze serpent on the staff. We have all been infected by the snake bite of sin. We have the promise of Jesus, "If I be lifted up from the earth (on the cross) I will draw all men unto me" (for salvation and healing) according to John 12: 32. On that cross, Jesus won the victory over that old serpent, the devil. He paid the penalty, for our redemption from the poison of sin and *also for our healing.*

The pole with the bronze serpent represents salvation from the enemy's destruction. The bent woman lived 18 years without knowing her Jewish **privilege** listed in Exodus 15: 26, Psalm 103: 1-3 and Psalm 91. Then she met Jesus. His compassionate, loving eyes were the first she looked into as He raised her up. The eyes of her Messiah, who said healing is the children's bread—the privilege of Abraham's seed. **Faith says what God says.**

Write 2 Chron. 16: 12-13.

✝

They Deserved It

The law brings wrath (Rom. 4: 15). The law brings **death** (2 Cor. 3:6). The letter of the law **kills**. But the Spirit gives **LIFE** (2 Cor. 3: 6).

I read those words many times, yet the meaning did not fully sink in until I heard Joseph Prince speak of how literally it was fulfilled in both the Old and New Testaments.

In Exodus chapter 32, when Moses brought the stone tablets down from the mountain, the law brought wrath. That very day, death came to some *three thousand* Hebrews. They had already made an idol, a golden calf to worship instead of the Living God. Beloved, t**hey DESERVED death.**

Contrast that with the day of Pentecost when the Holy Spirit first came upon the believers gathered in the upper room (Acts chapter 2). Peter immediately addressed the curious crowd and preached the first message of redemption through the cross of the Messiah.

That very day, the Spirit brought life and redemption to about *three thousand* added to the number of believers. **Beloved, they DID NOT DESERVE mercy**. Among them were some of the very Jews who had demanded just days earlier, "Crucify him."

Oh, the mercy of God.

The Spirit brings life, not death. **Faith says what God says.**

Write 2 Cor. 3: 6 in your prayer journal.

Birth Defects?

Who sinned, the man born blind, or his parents? The Jews assumed sin had to be the underlying cause, since they lived under the curse of the law which results in disease and blindness (Deut. 28: 15-64). Jesus said neither had sinned to cause the birth defect. He suggested the man's blindness was an opportunity for the glory of God (John 9:3). Some people will read that verse and assume that God *caused* the blindness so He would receive glory after opening the man's eyes. Not so. God permits defects because of the sin of Adam, but that is not, and *never* was, His perfect will, (John 10: 10; Jer. 32: 39-41). Every good and perfect gift comes down from above.

Adam's disobedience brought the curse of birth defects, disease, and death into the world. Jesus demonstrated He came to reverse the curse of the law of sin and death. That is the "works" He said **He must do in John 9:4--the works of reversing the curse**. That is the Good News He preached everywhere. Not just that we repent so we can go to heaven when we die. Yes, that is good news, but Jesus taught and demonstrated also that we can enjoy the Kingdom of Light's blessings here and now under the law of the Spirit of life in Christ Jesus (Rom. 8).

Example prayer:

Heavenly Father, Your word says I am a joint heir with Jesus Christ, born of His Spirit. As a member of His body, I do not inherit disease. The curse of any genetic problems is reversed in my body as I feed my spirit on Your Words of Life each day. Amen.

Testimony:

Pastor Jack Hayford was born with a birth defect. Doctors said the condition would eventually twist his neck and he would die. For five months, three times a week, Jack's mother took her baby for treatments to temporarily relieve his pain.

The doctor was so sure nothing could be done to correct it, he only charged her for six treatments even though he administered somewhere between 50 and 60. Jack's parents didn't know the Lord, but they heard about a Foursquare Church in Long Beach, California where Jesus healed people.

A relative took a note to the church and asked, "Will you pray for this baby?" The people said, "We will." The next day, Jack's parents began to notice changes.

Within the next few days, the doctor said, "This baby is well. There is nothing wrong with him."

Not only did the doctor declare Jack well, he refused to take the money for the few payments he was going to charge, because, he said, "I had nothing to do with the healing of this baby. This is something God did."- Pastor Jack Hayford's testimony.

Faith Says What God Says by Harriett Ford

†

Whose Family Genetics Do You Have?

The enemy kept reminding me of a genetic predisposition for certain health issues I might possibly experience due to my family history. Both my great-grandmother and my mother had skin cancers removed from their lips. Every time a suspicious area appeared, my first thought was the genetic code in my body.

Then one day the Holy Spirit impressed on me, You are a joint heir with Jesus Christ. The Father of spirits is your Father. Have you inherited disease from Him? You have been born again into the family of God (Rom. 8: 15).

Jesus is your elder brother (Heb. 2: 11). Does Jesus have skin cancer? Food allergies? Weak joints? Arthritis? Macular Degeneration? Hearing loss?' No, He does not. Immediately the Lord brought the First John 4: 17 verse to mind.

Praise God, I don't have to worry about genetic problems. **Faith says what God says.**

Write out the *second* half of First John 4: 17.

†

How Does The Devil Hurt God?

Nothing hurts a parent worse than to see his child suffering. Jesus said it is the Father's good **pleasure** to give You the kingdom (Luke 12:32). God takes delight in prospering you and does not wish to withhold any good thing from you (Psa. 84:11).

Satan's plan to hurt the Father is to rob Him of the **pleasure** He takes in His children. Premature death robs God of the pleasure, which He wanted for that precious life. Death is an enemy and causes Jesus to weep (see I Cor. 15: 26; John 11; 35 where death brought tears to the Messiah, even though He is the resurrection personified). That's how the devil hurts God.

Romans 4: 11 says you are created for God's pleasure. Nothing brings a parent greater joy than to see his children prosper and be in health even as their souls prosper (3 John, 2). So, what do we do when the thief tries to steal from us? We sharpen our sword of the spirit and cancel the plans of the enemy by speaking with the authority of Jesus' blood.

What words of authority are you speaking over your life? Curses Are Not God's Will!

Come now, let us reason together. I'm tired of the lies that blame God for human suffering. God received glory when Jesus *healed* the sick according to His will. That will has not changed.

Nobody ever said, "Praise the Lord, He struck me with cancer." If God struck people with disease then Jesus would be fighting against the Father by healing the illnesses. A kingdom divided against itself will not stand (Matt. 3:24).

Yes, there are Old Testament passages which indicate God caused disease, curses and plagues. God also provided a way of escape as in the bronze serpent on the pole (a type of the cross). **Under the law of the spirit of life, there are no diseases caused by God.** In the New Testament, the Lord struck down a grossly wicked person, Herod Agrippa in Acts 12: 23, but remember, Herod was living under the law of Moses. It was not God's will that Herod removed himself from the protection of obedience.

Think of it this way. I permitted my daughter to drive a car. She got into a traffic accident and was injured. Shards of glass remain embedded in her forehead even today. That was NOT my will. I permitted it by allowing her to drive. However, I *did not cause* it. I expected her to learn traffic safety laws and obey them.

Can God strike people with plagues and curses? If they choose not to learn his "safety laws and obey them," they are open to attack from the enemy. This is never God's will. And He always provides a way of escape. He has already done it. **Faith says what God says.**

Write Deut. 21: 23, Gal. 3: 13 and I Cor. 10: 13 in your journal.

†

Does God Scourge His Kids?
Commentary by Paul Ellis

For those whom the Lord loves He disciplines, and He scourges every son whom He receives. (Heb 12:6). *Is this good news?* An austere God Who punishes His children severely? That's how many see the Father. Because of this very common perception, I have paraphrased the following commentary by Paul Ellis.

Paul says the Father is not a severe, judgmental, scourging God: "How do I know? **I've seen Jesus.** He is none of these things. He is loving, gracious, kind and He desires to share his life with you. Jesus said he was about his Father's business—not about the condemning business but the redemption business."

How does scourging fit into this picture? It doesn't. It sticks out like a cobra in a kindergarten classroom. It shouldn't be there. Yet there it is, in black and white in Hebrews 12: 6.

That's what it says. The original Greek for scourges is *mastigoō*, the same word that describes what the soldiers did to Jesus (John 19:1). The Roman flagellum had bits of metal in the thongs and small hooks at the end called scorpions. Those hooks tore flesh from the body. Scourging was often fatal. "**I'm here to tell you that God never, ever, ever scourges his kids in such a brutal manner.** But before I give you my reasons, I have to be honest and admit that every single commentator I've read says He does. As far as I can tell, they all say stuff like this: *Scourges* means literally to flog or scourge… and entails any suffering which God ordains. Paul could also ask, how does scourging fit with the verse?

"Believers are not appointed to wrath." God's wrath has already been poured out on Jesus, and only His blood is redemptive, not ours. We cannot shed enough blood to atone for our sins. We are not qualified. We are not spotless, sinless lambs. **Paul Says It's a Misquote.** How dare anyone say there is a misquote in the perfect Word of God!?

Just look at the margin notes in your Bible. You will see that Hebrews 12: 5-6 is quoting Proverbs 3:11-12. It's a direct quote copied from the Old Testament and pasted into the New. Let's compare the original Proverbs version with the Hebrews version:

Original Quote From Prov 3:11-12

"My son, do not despise the chastening of the Lord,
Nor detest His correction;
For whom the Lord loves He corrects,
Just as a father the son in whom he delights."

Copied from Hebrews 12:5-6

"My son, do not make light of the Lord's discipline,
and do not lose heart when He rebukes you,
because the Lord disciplines the one He loves,

and He chastens everyone He accepts as His son."

The first three lines of the original Proverb are faithfully reproduced in Hebrews. But look at that last line. It is nothing like the original. How are we to account for this? One of them must be wrong.

What is the best translation of the Bible? It's not the Septuagint – it's Jesus! "The Son is the radiance of God's glory and the exact representation of his being…" (Heb 1:3).

I agree with Paul and with this quote from Pastor Bill Johnson's amazing ministry: *Jesus is perfect theology.* Paul asks, "What is Hebrews really saying? In my view, the Hebrew author of the epistle meant to say something like what we see in the proverb, namely: For whom the Lord loves he instructs, just as a father the son in whom he delights (Heb 12:6, my translation). This may be a better translation than the one in your English Bible because it satisfies three tests: (1) It is consistent with the revelation of God the Father given to us through Jesus the Son, (2) it is consistent with many other scriptures indicating that God delights in His children and that He cares enough to bring life-giving correction, and (3) it fits the context of Hebrews 12.

Many people will disagree and point to Old Testament examples to support their argument that God pours scourging wrath on His children to correct them. Aren't you glad Jesus gave us a "new and better covenant" (Heb. 8: 6)? **Write Hebrews 8: 6.**

†

Paul's Thorn

Paul's thorn in the flesh was clearly a messenger of Satan who buffeted him with persecution everywhere he preached. Paul asked God for relief, and God gave him sufficient grace to endure it.

Plainly, God did not stop the persecution, because he gave man dominion and does not stop wicked men from afflicting Christians, or He would have been stopping their free will. In 2 Cor. 11: 26-27, Paul lists a whole string of sufferings inflicted by men, which he calls "my infirmities" in verse 30—the same word he uses describing the thorn.

I studied this out for myself, and later found it in Andrew Wommack's messages, which was confirmation to me that I was hearing from the Holy Spirit. You can type in your browser, Paul's thorn in the flesh, and Andrew's full teaching will come up. Below is a paragraph from Andrew. If we look at the context of Paul's thorn in the flesh, we find that infirmity does not mean sickness in 2 Corinthians 12:9 and 10. In 2 Corinthians 11:30, Paul uses the exact terminology of "glorying in infirmities" that is used just a few verses later in speaking about this thorn.

In the eleventh chapter he had just finished listing what those infirmities were. In verses 23-29, he lists such things as imprisonment, stripes, shipwrecks, and stoning; none of these speak of sickness.

Verse 27 mentions weakness and painfulness, which some have tried to make mean sickness, but it is just as possible he could have been weary and suffered painfulness from such things as being stoned and left for dead (Acts 14:19). All these things listed in 2 Corinthians 11 refer to persecutions as "infirmities." So, in context, Paul's thorn was a demonic angel or messenger sent by Satan which continually stirred up persecution against him.

This is also verified by three Old Testament references (Num. 33:55; Josh. 23:13 and Judg. 2:3), where people are spoken of as being "thorns in your sides" and "thorns in your eyes."—Andrew Wommack. Think about this. Why would a commander strike one his own generals with a disease of the flesh?

People even took *handkerchiefs* and aprons that had touched *Paul's* body, and they carried them to everyone who was sick. All of the sick people were healed (Acts 19: 12). He himself was healed of blindness and later also raised from the dead after being stoned in Acts 14: 19. With such a powerful anointing, how could the thief torment him with illness? Anyone who thinks God sent them a thorn in the flesh needs to ask himself, *have I had an abundance of supernatural revelation from God? Have I visited heaven as Paul did?* You find Pauls' frame of reference for the thorn is always human enemies inspired by the messenger of Satan. See Numbers 33:55. See also Joshua 23:13 and Judges 2:3.

Satan's messenger stirred up riots and caused people to persecute Paul everywhere he traveled. Paul's blindness was temporary. His injuries from three brutal whippings and a stoning no doubt left significant scars. But his suffering was not inflicted by God. Instead, God gave him sufficient grace to overcome it, and also healed him many times (Acts 14: 19-23).

It is clear that God does not stop persecution, because He never imposes His will on any one. However, people can afflict themselves by unhealthy, addictive, unforgiving, and sinful lifestyles. Even then, Jesus is always willing to forgive and to heal a sincerely repentant heart. **Faith says what God says.**

Write Joel 3: 10 and Psalm 27: 13.
Speak those words over your own life, regardless of how weak you feel.

†

Sharing In Christ's Suffering?

I Pet. 4: 12: "Beloved, do not be surprised at the fiery trial that has come upon you, as though something strange were happening to you. 13: But rejoice that you share in the sufferings Christ, so you may be overjoyed at the revelation of His glory. 14: If you are insulted for the name of Christ, you are blessed, because the Spirit of glory and of God rests on you."

I have heard it said that a person who is suffering a painful illness is *"sharing* in Christ's suffering." I asked the Lord, "Did You ever suffer a painful illness?"

He never did. Not until He became our substitute on the cross when He took all painful illnesses into His own body (Isa.53: 4 and I Pet. 2: 24).

Scriptures are very clear that the fiery trials and suffering which Jesus, Peter, and James speak of is persecution. In Matthew 13: 21, Jesus spells it out plainly. "Tribulation and persecution are because of the Word."

People who live godly lives are **NEVER** promised illness under the new covenant. They are targets for the enemy, who hates Christians. See John 10: 10.

If you have been taught you are "sharing in Christ's suffering" with an illness sent for you to learn patience or humility, you will never resist the works of the devil, who comes to steal your health, kill your soul, and destroy your life (John 10: 10).

If you are waiting on God to heal your body someday when He gets around to it, you are not actively resisting the thief. How do you do that?

Be a diligent seeker. Learn how to exercise the authority Jesus gave you.

Make this your confession of faith today:

I am sowing the healing words into my mind and spirit. I am Meditating on the healing verses night and day, (Josh. 1: 8). If I only sow a small seed, I get only a small harvest. Who wants to be only 30 percent healed? I will continue to sow these verses into the good soil of my heart until I receive a hundred-fold harvest of health.

†

Tempted To Give Up?

Where is your fighting spirit? At times you may be tempted to give up, but you are not defeated. Do you know the devil can tempt us to go home before out time? However, we are NOT going until God is finished with our lives—not unless we allow it.

Continue to plan for your future. When I went in for a bilateral mastectomy in 1993, I had extensions put in my hair so it would look nice while I was hospitalized. Not out of vanity, (well a little) but because I was planning to go back to my job as soon as possible. I continued to act in faith that I would live a long life as promised in Psalm 91. I refused chemo and radiation. I planned to be well. I am still well today.

Example prayer:

Father, I thank You that I have hope and a future, and it does not include disease. I pray as the believers prayed in Acts 4: 30: "Stretch forth Your hand to heal and glorify the Name of Your Son Jesus." I receive that healing from Your hand for the glory of Jesus and I minister healing to others for Your glory to others. Amen.

Testimony:

If Satan cannot kill you with disease, he will resort to lies. An evil spirit manifested itself to Evangelist Tim Thompson one night. It appeared as the virgin Mary (2 Cor. 11: 14) and began to speak to him, saying, "I know how you have struggled. I know how tired you are. The Lord says you can come home now."

The spirit enticed him to take his own life and promised to hold him lovingly him until he died. Tim immediately recognized the spirit, whose actual name is Suicide. He commanded it to leave in Jesus' Name. The spirit left him.

As a former psychic and Satanic priest, Tim has denounced all ties with the demonic spirit world. He is now a highly respected minister of deliverance, reaching out to people who have been ensnared in witchcraft, Satanism, and the occult world.

†

A Broken Promise?

Have you ever made a promise to God and you did not keep it? I have. Ecclesiastes 5: 6 says "Don't let your mouth make you sin. And don't defend yourself by telling the Temple messenger that the promise you made was a mistake. That would make God angry, and he might wipe out everything you have achieved."

While I was making my bed, which strangely is where the Holy Spirit sometimes speaks, I was repenting for a promise I had made and broken. I felt very sad, and I wondered if I had made God so angry that He might wipe me out. How would He deal with me? He reminded me instantly that Peter once *made a promise* to the Lord, that even if he had to die with Jesus, he would never disown Him (Matt. 26: 35). He broke that promise three times that very night.

Did Jesus punish Peter? Wipe him out? Destroy everything he had achieved?

No. He simply asked Peter to acknowledge his love, three times. One time for every denial. What a gentle and loving call back to the ministry for which Peter had been trained. No punishment, not even a rebuke. Jesus did not come to condemn the world, but to save it. He knows we humans are dust and are going to fail. That's why He has already paid the penalty for us and for our broken promises.

Father, I am so glad I can come to the throne in the righteous robe of Jesus and find mercy, grace and forgiveness. You don't want us to continually remind You of our failures and sins, which You said You will not remember. Instead, You want us to put You in remembrance of Your word, so that you can bless us as You blessed Peter. Jesus did not even ask him to repent. Instead, He asked Peter to remind Him of the love he had for him. That is restorative love that overcomes all things and faith works by love. I love You, Lord. Amen.

†

Receive From The Spirit, Not The Flesh

God is Spirit. He speaks to the inner man, the spirit man where His incorruptible seed dwells (I John 3: 9) and when you can receive from any man's *regenerated spirit* (your teacher, pastor, friend, or even your mother) instead of looking at the natural man—the imperfect flesh in which dwells no good thing—you can receive what the Holy Spirit is teaching.

God wants you to receive revelation from your *own* regenerated spirit. It takes meditation and commitment, but victory is **promised**. Every promise is yes and amen, (2 Cor. 1: 20). Do not settle for less.

You can know you have victory with complete confidence, because your faith is based solely on the Word of God, not on man's reasoning, imperfect understanding, or other people's experiences. His incorruptible seed dwells in your reborn spirit. Daily get in touch with Him in the secret place of Psalm 91 for these truths to become reality in your life.

Write a promise from Psalm 91 that speaks to your greatest concern.

†

Isn't Doubt Always Present?

One woman in my Bible study group asked me about having doubt when we pray for healing.

"Don't we all have a little doubt at times? And will doubt cancel my faith?"

It is in the heart that we must have no doubt. The heart is the new-creation part of our being where the Holy Spirit dwells. That's why we must guard our hearts with all diligence. That's where the faith seed is planted. We want it to produce a harvest of faith, not doubt.

In the natural mind, which must be renewed daily to things of the spirit, we often have a little doubt present. But that is easily remedied. Pull the doubt weeds! Nourish the faith seeds.

Remember the father of the little boy with seizures? He said, "Lord I do believe. Help me where faith fails." He had little faith, but he also had *enough* faith. Jesus healed his son.

Faith comes by hearing and hearing (continually) by the Word. Read it. Take it like medicine, several times a day. Speak it aloud to your body. Hear your own voice speaking God's word. It will not return to Him empty of the purpose for which He sends it. **Faith says what God says.**

Write Matt. 17: 20. Speak it over your life.

†

Words Can Make It Go

This meditation is a reminder. If you walk only by natural sun light, you will only have natural results.

Jesus used supernatural words to change the natural things around him. Both Mark 11:13-14 and 20-24 tell how He withered the fig tree with words.

This wasn't limited to a tree. He used a mountain as an example. But the **mountain is symbolic of any challenge in your life.** He was making the point that we also can use words, speak with our mouths and believe in our hearts and we can have what we say. Do you doubt that? I didn't say it. The Lord did.

Your words affect the natural as well as the spiritual world. That mountain got there by words (Genesis Chapter One). **Words can make it go.** This is supernatural Son Light (revelation knowledge).

My husband John and I spoke life to a dying redbud tree one spring, and it bloomed. I spoke life to my asthmatic cat and he is healthy. I did not beg God to do it. I spoke life in Jesus' name. I speak life and health to my body, soul, and spirit every day.

When symptoms come, I resist them by the blood of the Lamb. They may hang around for a while, but they must leave in Jesus' Name as I continue to resist. This is not to say that I ignore sound medical advice or pretend the symptoms to do not exist. It is to say that I deny those symptoms the right to stay. **Faith says what God**

says.

Write James 4: 7-8 and speak these words over your life.

Testimony:

I received the message below from a lady in my Bible study group: My husband complained that his chest was hurting. I spoke to the pain in the name of Jesus like you taught us. The pain left. Praise God. – D. D.

What You Focus On Will Magnify!

Whatever you focus on is what you will magnify. This is so important that I have repeated the teaching. Peter *saw* Jesus walking on the water. He asked the Lord to bid him come. He heard Jesus say, "Come." Peter stepped out of the boat and walked on the water (Matt. 14: 22-33), quite literally walking on the Word, *come.* That is supernatural still today.

However, Peter stopped *looking* at Jesus on the storm-tossed Sea of Galilee. Why? As a professional fisherman, Peter knew the sea very well. He knew that the wind and waves would not support him. He *looked* at the strong wind and waves. They were real. He was terrified and began to sink.

That is a natural fact still today.

If you want to walk above the natural facts, you have to keep your eye on the Word. The natural facts are real. A diagnosis can be as terrifying as strong wind and waves. But facts are subject to change by the unchangeable, settled-forever-in-heaven Word of God.

Psalm 101: 3 says, "I will not set my eyes on worthless things." (Some TV programs come to mind.) Other things like doctor's reports could be included as "worthless things" when we renew our minds to God's word on healing. Not that we ignore sound medicine, but we do not give place to a medical forecast that disagrees with God's promise, which says we will come to the grave at a full old age.

Write Job 5: 26, Psa. 91: 16, and Psa. 92: 14. Meditate on these verses. Speak these verses to any medical report that says differently.

†

The Unseen World

You've heard this before. It bears repeating. The Bible speaks of two invisible kingdoms which are currently in operation here in the earth (Col. 1: 13). Jesus called Satan the god of this world in John 12: 31, and also the ruler of the kingdom of darkness. Jesus said that the kingdom of Light is not visible outwardly but is "within you," (Luke 17: 21-22).

Jesus also said that the Father will love those who keep His commands. He added, "I too will love them and will **manifest** myself" to them, (Jn 14: 21-24). How do the Father and Son manifest in our lives? Some see visions of the Lord and His angels. Some experience His presence in a tangible, supernatural event (Acts 2: 4). In His earthly ministry, Jesus demonstrated also that the Father wants to manifest His kingdom in the health and well-being of His followers (John 5:19; 10:10). He said "Seek ye first the kingdom of God and His righteousness and all these things will be added to you," (Matt. 6: 33). When you seek Him, the Kingdom will manifest in blessings.

Hyper-intellectuals usually deny the existence of any spirit world. Then there are people who actually seek the kingdom of darkness—ghost hunters, demon chasers, spiritualists, mediums, and Satanists. The dark kingdom will manifest for them also. The evil rulers of the unseen world, described in Ephesians 6: 12, are deceiving spirits. They steal kingdom blessings every day from people who do not know how to exercise their spiritual authority.

Read Lev. 19: 31 and Isa. 8: 19. If you have dabbled in the occult in any form--Ouija boards, astrology, horoscopes, spiritualism, fortune tellers, mediums, etc.—repent and write your prayer, renouncing them and breaking those ties. Ask the Lord to sweep through your spirit and cleanse you of all unrighteousness.

†

Portals That Open To Darkness

Testimony:

I began seeking the Lord earnestly as a young woman. After months of reading and praying, I got down on my knees at home one night. The Lord's presence overwhelmed me in a powerful and tangible manner.

That wondrous supernatural awareness assured me forever, *Jesus is real*. I had been born into His spiritual kingdom of Light. God became the Father of my spirit. Not long after, I also became aware that the kingdom darkness is equally real.

I had previously given no thought to the devil. He was irrelevant.

Just graduated from college at that time, we had no furniture. My mother-in-law donated a wicker settee and two chairs, which I covered with a jungle print at her suggestion. In keeping with the jungle theme, I bought a few African figures carved from black wood and placed them on a book shelf. Shortly after I received the baptism of the Holy Spirit, I noticed these figures lying face down on the floor. I picked them up several times, wondering how they got knocked down. Finally, I realized they were somebody's idols. I got rid of them at once.

Deuteronomy 7: 26 says, "Neither shalt thou **bring**

an abomination **into** thine house, lest thou be a cursed thing like it: but thou shalt utterly detest it, and thou shalt utterly abhor it; for it is a cursed thing. ... **Do not bring** any of these **idols into your homes**, or the same curse will be on you that is on them." (KJV). I soon discovered this warning also includes certain music, movies, and books. I got rid of them too.

Do you have items, knick knacks, souvenirs (like Buddha idols), or even a Ouija board that are defined by scripture as "cursed things"? What should you do with them?

†

Are You A Snake Handler?

Whenever I see a snake, I run the other way, like Moses did when his rod became a snake for the first time (Ex. 4: 3). It's a repulsive creature.

The deadly black mamba in Africa is a perfect symbol for Satan. It has no other purpose but to kill and destroy life. A grown man will die from its venom. Often in less than twenty minutes. God said He would put enmity between the woman's seed and the serpent's seed. What are these seeds? Forty-four verses in the New Testament refer to the Word of God as seed.

We know that Satan is a spirit being. He has no physical seed capable of reproducing physical bodies on the earth. We know that Jesus is the Word made flesh, a life-giving spirit come down from above (I Cor. 15: 45).

The word-seed spoken to Mary created a physical body for Jesus in the likeness of human flesh. The Word-seed produces a harvest of life in abundance for those who sow it, get it deeply rooted, and nurture it. God has an enemy whose servants are also sowing seed in the Master's field (Matt. 13: 28-30). Satan's word-seeds are lies that question the authority of God's word (Gen 3: 1). They will also produce a harvest—a harvest of loss, destruction, and death. (John 10: 10).

Which seeds are planted in the garden of your heart? Who told you that you won't get well, or that you will stay impoverished, lonely, defeated? Not God.

The often-misinterpreted scripture in Mark 16: 18 and Luke 10: 19 about power to tread on serpents and scorpions actually means divine authority over the enemy, who is named in Revelation 12: 9 as "that old serpent the devil." The verse about taking up serpents is not meant for deliberately handling deadly snakes in order to prove your faith. That's putting God to a foolish test. **Faith says what God says.**

Declare there is healing in the atonement for all three parts of your triune being: body, soul, and spirit (I Thess. 5: 23).

Example prayer:

Father, You said to Moses, "Make a snake and mount it on a pole. When anyone who is bitten looks at it, he will live." (Numbers 21: 8).

I see that Jesus won the complete victory over the snake bite of sin when He became sin for us and was nailed to the cross. When I look at Him, and the power of His blood, I know that I will live and not die. Thank You, Jesus. Amen.

What Makes God's Word Of None Effect?

A startling thought. Can God's Word become ineffective? Really?

We believe that our sovereign God can do all things. We do not like to think His power is limited. However, Jesus said in John 12: 40, "Their eyes are blinded, their hearts are hardened, so that they can neither see with their eyes, nor understand with their hearts, nor turn—and I would HEAL them."

Do you see that? He would heal them. He wanted to, but He could not!

"Woe to you scribes and lawyers! For ye have taken away the **key** of knowledge" (Luke 11: 52). In essence, "You have obscured and destroyed the true knowledge," which is a key to the kingdom.

Jesus said in effect, "By your wrong interpretations of Scripture, you have filled people with strong prejudices against the gospel, so you not only reject it yourselves, but hinder others from receiving it (Luke 11: 52).

"You nullify the word of God by tradition, making it of none effect," (Mark 7: 12).What does it take to get on the other side of that false teaching that just because somebody got sick and died, it must have been God's will? Lazarus got sick and died prematurely. Was that Gods' will? No, or Jesus would have been acting contrary to the Father's will by raising Lazarus.

It is the enemy who blinds minds, hardens hearts, steals good years, and hurts God in this manner. Yes, God is hurt by death. He wept at the tomb of Lazarus. Even though He had already decreed that Lazarus should be raised (John 11: 4). He wept.

Was He weeping out of sympathy for the grieved? Possibly, He was also grieved by the unbelief present. Some of those very people had evil, hardened hearts. They ran to the chief priests to report what had happened that very day. in order to have Him arrested. These People saw Lazarus come out of the grave. Yet, their eyes were blinded and their hearts were hardened.

Example prayer:

Father I come to Your throne of grace and ask You to remove any spiritual blindness from my eyes. I ask for renewed understanding of Your goodness and mercy. I come agreeing with Martha, that Jesus is the Messiah, the Son of God. Lord Jesus, You are the Resurrection and the life. I come to You to receive resurrection-life in my spirit, soul and body today. I come to glorify Your name forever. Amen.

Grace Does Not Speak Thorn Language

Who is the accuser who daily throw thorns and fiery darts at us, reminding us of our weaknesses, our failures, our rebellion, our sins?

Who dares to contradict the Word of the Lord that says we ARE the very righteousness of God in Christ, which has been imputed to us (2 Cor. 5: 21)? Who dares to steal our peace (mental soundness) our right standing with God (forgiveness), or the health of our physical body (Psalm 103: 4)?

Who told you that you are not worthy to be healed (Matt. 8: 8)? Not Jesus.

Grace always triumphs over the law of sin and death. The Father does not want to remember your sins, once you have confessed and turned away (Heb. 8: 12). He wants to be put into remembrance of His Word so that He can bless you (Isa. 43: 26).

Write Rev. 12: 10; John 8: 11; and I John 1: 8-10. Speak God's words of grace and mercy over your life. Not the thorny words of the accuser.

Example Prayer:

Father, I don't always feel righteous, but Your Word declares that righteousness is not something I do. It is something I am. I refuse to listen to thorn

language from the accuser. Thank you for Your mercy, new every morning (Lam. 3: 22-23), because I used up yesterdays' mercy. Amen.

†

What's Your Heart Language?

"As a man thinks in his heart, so is he," (Proverbs 23:7). What are you thinking in your heart today? Has the enemy injected fear, doubt, anxiety? Do you see yourself living in defeat and distress? Are you speaking a language of victory or defeat? You can control the thoughts in your mind and build a new picture in your heart. It takes effort, but you do not have to entertain thoughts that cause stress. First Peter 5: 7 says to cast all your anxieties on Him, because He cares for you. Get a picture of yourself as a joint heir with Jesus Christ, redeemed, healed, set free, walking in victory and praising God.

"And the LORD said, Behold, the people *is* one, and they have all one language; and this they begin to do: and now nothing will be restrained from them which they *have imagined* to do," (Gen. 11: 6). This verse refers to the tower of Babel and has layers of meaning. However, if we as believers can renew our imaginations to conform to His will, we have even greater power to do what we imagine. Believers should have one language. The language of faith which works by love. Don't hesitate to use it. **Faith says what God says.**

Write Num. 22: 38 and Isa. 59: 21. Whose words are you going to speak? My God is not Cruel, Sorry About Yours

†

The Universal Question: Why Do Bad Things Happen To Good People?

Rabbi Harold Kushner says he no longer hold God responsible for illnesses, accidents, and natural disasters, because: "I realize that I lose so much when I blame God for those things.

I can worship a God who hates suffering but cannot eliminate it, more easily than I can worship a God who chooses to make children suffer and die, for whatever exalted reason.

In response to the *God is Dead* movement back in the 1960s, I remember seeing a bumper sticker that read, 'My God is not dead; sorry about yours.'

I guess my bumper sticker reads, 'My God is not cruel; sorry about yours.' God does not cause our misfortunes."Some misfortunes are caused by bad people, bad weather, bad choices we make, and some are simply an inevitable consequence of our being fallible human beings living in a world ruled by Satan.I agree with Rabbi Kushner:

"The painful things that happen to us are not punishments for our misbehavior. (Jesus already took that punishment.) Because the tragedy is not God's will, we need not feel hurt or betrayed by God when tragedy strikes. We can turn to Him for help in overcoming it, precisely because we can tell ourselves that God is as outraged by it as we are."

The wonderful thing is, God expects us to be overcomers, just as Jesus is. And He equips us with the power of the blood, the Holy Spirit, and the word of our testimony. **Faith says what God says.**

Write I Cor. 10: 13 and Jeremiah 29: 11. Example prayer: Father, I see a world which reaps the consequences of sin and death every day. When tragedy strikes, I know that in the beginning this was never Your plan. There is no tragedy, sorrow, or disaster in heaven. You said Your plans are to do good and not evil to Your people. You have made a way of escape for people who trust in Your righteousness. When I feel lost in the darkness of devastating events, light the way and lead me in it. Equip me with the wisdom and power I need to overcome the darkness, so that Your will is done on earth as it is in heaven. Amen.

†

How Does Satan Speak?

Satan is a spirit. He communicates to people through the spirit of the mind, just as he spoke to Adam and Eve and also to Jesus.

As contrary as it seems, the enemy sometimes **speaks** through family and well-meaning believers.

Remember Jesus **said** to Peter, "Get thee behind me Satan," (Matt. 16: 23) after Peter tried to convince Him not to surrender without a fight.

Remember what Mrs. Job said to her husband. "You might as well curse God and die." Those awful words were almost a direct quote from Satan in Job 1: 11.

What are your family members saying to you? Julia's friends thought she was delusional. See below.

Testimony:

"Friends, I am writing to praise God for my miraculous healing (of a tremendously painful and medically incurable disease). The disease and its symptoms did not leave my body all at once, but I hold fast to my confession of faith that by His stripes I am healed."

Julia's friends thought she was delusional when she continued to say "I am healed by Jesus' stripes," (that's faith-talk) because her body was obviously so weak, her pain so great, the lesions on her flesh so gross. One woman even advised, "Instead, why don't you say you *hope* God will heal you."

But Julia had learned that hope is not faith, and there is power in the spoken word. After fifteen months, Julia's rheumatologist said, "We find only a trace of the myositis left in your muscles." \

He seemed stumped by her amazing progress. He also commented that five other doctors had agreed with his diagnosis. Julia thought to herself, "Jesus didn't agree with the doctors! Jesus declared in His Word that by His stripes, I am healed!!!" – Julia Frazier White.

Julia's full testimony can be found at Gillis Triplett: How I Overcame an Incurable Disease!
https://www.gillistriplett.com/healing/articles/incurable.html

†

He Will Show You Things To Come

The Spirit of Truth was a mystery to me until I began to experience His presence. He truly does bring to my remembrance the words of Jesus (John 16: 12-14) when I am speaking to someone. I discovered that He leads me into all Truth when I run across doctrinal error. And yes, He has shown me things to come (John 16: 13).

In the year 2000, I was making my bed when I heard three words in my spirit: Wreck, Death, Scott. Scott is my younger brother's name. I fell to my knees and begged God for his life. I pledged to pray daily for his life. But it was as if the Lord hit a delete key in my mind. I did *not remember* the words until a few months after Scott was killed in a car wreck on Christmas Eve.

Devastated, I searched the scriptures about Jesus' prophetic words, fearing I had failed in a prayer assignment. I discovered that many times the apostles did not understand until after the words were fulfilled (Luke 18: 34). The meaning was "*hidden* from them."

The Holy Spirit comforted me. I could not have prevented the accident that took Scott's life. The prophecy was hidden from me until after the accident.

I could, however, intercede for my daughter, when the Lord gave me a specific word involving her car wreck before it happened. She survived her injuries, recovered, and even walked without the "drop foot" her surgeon had predicted she would have. Thanks be to the Holy Spirit's warning.

Father, why could one accident have been fatal and the other not? I don't know. You have secrets. You have mysteries (Deut. 29: 29). I do know this. You are good. You are love. The Spirit of Truth will lead me into all truth, show me things to come, and comfort me. Amen. **Faith says what God says.**

Can you think of a time when that inner voice spared you from danger? Write it in your prayer journal.

†

Left At The Mercy Of Satan?

"I will not leave you as orphans," John 14: 18. Wow, was I ever taught wrong. How shocking to learn that Satan is the god of this world, according to Jesus' own words in John 12: 31. I thought God was totally in control of everything on earth. Silly me.

He could certainly do a lot better job of controlling the planet than what we see on the news every day. How abandoned the disciples must have felt when our Lord said He was going to the Father. Would God really leave them (and us) here to struggle through life at the mercy of Satan (2 Cor. 4: 4)? Would He really leave us defenseless? Is there no benefit to being translated from the dominion of the kingdom of darkness (Col. 1: 13) **until *after* we die and go to heaven?**

Thank God, Jesus didn't leave us without supernatural comfort. He didn't leave us without supernatural authority. He didn't leave us without the power of His Name. He didn't leave us without weapons of spiritual warfare.

The Spirit of Truth is here with us to comfort, teach, and lead us into all truth. His mission is described in John 14, 15, 16 and throughout the book of Acts.

Thank God that greater and more powerful is He that is in me than the god of this world. Thank God, I have spiritual weapons of warfare, mighty to the pulling down of strongholds (Eph. 6: 10-20). **Faith says what**

God says.

Write three things the Holy Spirit does for us based on what Jesus said in John chapters 14, 15, 16. Start speaking them over your life. Write down what supernatural things are beginning to happen in your life. Example prayer: Lord, You said the Holy Spirit will guide me into all truth and bring to my remembrance Your words. You said He will show me things to come. Thank You for supernatural guidance. I receive it every day in Your Name. Amen.

†

The Holy Spirit Quickens Our Mortal Bodies

Romans 8: 11 says the Holy Spirit makes alive your mortal body. Most people read that verse and think of the resurrection. It does mean that. It also means this: when the Holy Spirit dwells in us and the word dwells in us richly, He makes alive our mortal flesh in the land of the living (Psalm 27: 13). His life in us drives out disease from our bodies. That is good news!

It is the Father's good pleasure to give the Holy Spirit to those who **ask** Him and are seeking Him first for Who He is and not just for what He can do for them (Matt. 7: 11; Luke 11: 13). He wants His children to see the goodness of the Lord in the land of the living.He won't give you a stone for bread or a snake for fish.

Have you asked for the baptism of the Holy Spirit? Write Luke 3: 16 and Luke 11: 13 here and speak these verses over your life.

Example prayer:

Father, I ask you for the baptism of the Holy Spirit, according to Luke 11: 13. I believe You are filling me (Mark 1: 8). I believe the Holy Spirit is my teacher, guide, and comforter according to John chapters 14 and 15. And I receive the manifestation of the Spirit according to John 14: 21-22; Acts 2:4; 10:46; and 19:6. I believe the Spirit quickens my

mortal body and drives out disease today. Praise and thanksgiving fill my heart. Amen.

†

Wrinkle-Free Garment?

My mom was a fantastic seamstress. She sewed most of my school clothes, prom dresses, and even my beautiful wedding gown. She always looked for a certain fabric blend of two materials that remained wrinkle-free.

Two passages in the Mosaic Law forbid the wearing of different types of fabric; that is, the wearing of blended fabrics—those woven from two different materials, (Lev. 19: 19).

I asked the Lord to show me the meaning of this, because whenever He stresses anything twice, it is important.

God woke me this morning and downloaded this to my heart. A garment is for covering. Adam lost his garment of righteousness and Jesus restored it to us. A princely garment of righteousness. This garment must **not be a blend of self-righteousness and God's righteousness.** It must be seamless, like the robe Jesus wore.

What a wonderful understanding. I don't have to earn God's favor by my own works. Only by receiving the righteousness of God by faith in the atonement can I wear the proper garment to the throne of Grace and the wedding supper of the Lamb.

This robe is not just a cover-up. It is a clean-up. Now I am equipped to do righteous works by the power of

His spirit operating in me. **Faith says what God says.**

Write Isaiah 64: 6 and Luke 15: 22. Rejoice! Your Father has a robe of righteousness for you.

†

Which Robe Are You Wearing?

God stresses the story of the robe, so I do not hesitate to repeat it. God crowned Adam with glory and honor, however he lost his garment of glory when he sinned.

Joseph, as a type of Christ, had a special coat given to him by his father. That caused his brothers to hate him, plan to kill him, and dip his coat in animal blood to take to the father. That is a shadow of how our Lord's own Jewish brothers hated him (John 1: 11). Jacob believed his son Joseph was dead because of the blood stains on his coat, yet Jacob lived to be reunited with Joseph in Egypt one day—a type of the resurrection.

Someone, perhaps Mary, wove a special seamless robe for Jesus and He wore it to the cross. He lost His special garment also. He was actually stripped naked when they nailed Him to the cross.

Nakedness in the Bible always represents loss of covering for sin. Like the first Adam, Jesus lost His covering when He became the sin of the whole world.

We cannot come to the throne of Grace if we are wearing a robe of self-righteousness. We can only come in the seamless robe of Jesus' righteousness, which is imputed to us by faith. We cannot come wearing Peter's righteousness, or Paul's. Or any other holy person, because none of them shed perfect blood to present to the Father for our sins. There is only One

Faith Says What God Says by Harriett Ford

Mediator between God and man (I Tim. 2: 5).

The seamless robe? Well, you know the story. The sinners gambled for it.

Good news. Those who receive Jesus get to put on the robe of Christ's righteousness (Zech. 3: 4; Rev. 19: 13). They don't have to gamble for it and take a chance on losing it. It is a promise. **Faith says what God says.**

Write Zech. 3: 4 and Luke 15: 22. Imagine yourself wearing this garment.

†

What Jesus Alone Can Do

So very sincerely, the grandfather prayed. Now in his 90s, he humbly asked God to put the cancer on him instead of his little two-year-old great-granddaughter, who had been undergoing treatment for several months.

He prayed that he could take the disease in her place. That she would live and not die. As soon as I heard that sad story in my Bible study group, the Lord whispered, "That is what I did for my people. I bore their sicknesses."

We are not qualified to pay for another person's sins, or to bear their sicknesses. Jesus is the only One Who was qualified to do that. Praise God, He has already done it. **Faith says what God says.**

Write out Isa. 53:4-5 and Matt. 8: 16-17. Is physical healing mentioned in either verse?

†

Layers Of Meaning

There are Layers of meaning in the treasure of God's Word--historic, symbolic, prophetic, and personal.

Here is a perfect example. There stood a well in the field, and flocks of sheep were lying there beside it, for from that well the shepherds watered the flocks.

"Now the stone on the mouth of the well was large. When all the flocks were gathered there, the shepherds would then roll the stone from the mouth of the well and water the sheep, and put the stone back in its place on the mouth of the well." (Gen. 29: 3).

This is a historic account of Jacob coming to a well and meeting his future bride, Rachel (Gen. 29: 10). He rolled the stone away and watered the flocks for Rachel.

Jacob disregarded the rule of the well; and at the risk of incurring the wrath of the local herdsmen and shepherds. By a feat of great personal strength, he removed unaided the stone covering, and offered to Rachel the service of watering Laban's flock.

This stone is also a prophetic picture of the empty tomb after the large stone had been <u>rolled away</u> by the angels. Since that day, the sheep of Christ's fold—His future bride—can be watered with Living Water, (John 7: 38; Acts chapter one).

Example prayer:

Father, I thank You for the joy of drawing Living Water from the well of salvation, (Isa. 12: 3). As Your bride, I will give a cup of cold water to Your thirsting people wherever I meet them, that they may share in the Life of Jesus (John 1: 4). Fill me to overflowing, Holy Spirit, that I may share a cup of cold water with someone who is thirsty. Amen.

Testimony:

My friend Robin Walsh saw a homeless person on the streets of Springfield, Missouri. Robin felt impressed to take her a cup of ice water, as it was a hot summer day. At the drive-through, she ordered not one, but four waters not knowing why. Robin ended up ministering to four thirsty street people that day. Like the apostles, she had no money to give them, but by direction of the Holy Spirit, she gave what she had—the life-giving words of Jesus.

✝

Separating Truth From Lies

Demons lie through false religions, psychics, mediums, misguided church-goers etc. to convince people that even without Christ there is life after death and some place of peaceful existence. The truth is that it is impossible to spend eternity anywhere but Hell for those who refuse to accept Jesus as their Savior from sin (John 14: 6).

There is no other name under heaven whereby men might be saved, (Acts 4: 12). Not Buddha. Not Allah. Not Confucius. Not Krishna.

No matter how sincere a worshiper may be, no matter how peaceful and prayerful, the Bible is quite clear. No man comes to the Father except through the Son (John 14: 6).

I used to think that because faith comes by hearing, if I heard, read, and studied the Word, I would eventually build enough faith to have more victory when praying for the sick. That is partly true. Then the Lord began to show me how the enemy also deceives by keeping us focused only on the natural, reasonable, possible realm.

Demons will lie and say, "How can anyone be healed because of Jesus' stripes 2000 some years ago?" The answer is, "Because it is written. God's word is true, and every promise in the book is yea and amen."

Example prayer:

Father, I thank You that You are not a man that You should lie. I thank You that Your word cuts away lies from the truth in my renewed mind. I thank You that the Holy Spirit always agrees with Your word. His power lives in me and quickens (makes alive) my flesh. I receive that quickening daily, In Jesus' Name. Amen.

†

Something Of Substance

Faith has substance, according to Hebrews. 11: 1. Faith has in it the substance (the physical reality) of things hoped for.

The definition of substance is "that of which a thing consists; physical matter or material."

Abraham called into existence what he hoped for, a child. That child did not yet exist in the physical world. His faith activated the promise. Romans 4: 17 says "before God in Whom he believed, He called those things which did not exist as though they did." *He believed first without having to see it.* He did not need something tangible, something he could see and touch.

God had promised him that he would be the father of many nations. God's Word was enough. He and Sara received their impossible-miracle son Isaac when they were well beyond child-bearing years.

Why did they have to wait so long? Because Isaac's birth was in the realm of the supernatural. It was a type of Christ's birth. Sometimes God allows impossible circumstances, so that when His Word prevails, all glory goes to Him.

Example prayer:

Father, You said all things are possible to them who believe. I am a believer. I am not satisfied to do

what I can achieve merely in my own strength, for then You do not get the glory. I invite You to work Your mighty works to bless others through the weakness of my human flesh. Amen

†

Beyond Understanding

A click on the computer screen shows amazing photos of the galaxies and the infinite numbers of stars in the heavens. Psalm 147: 4 says that God counts the stars and calls them all by name. This is beyond human understanding.

We cannot begin to count the stars in even our closest galaxies. God also knows the very number of hairs on our heads. This also is beyond understanding. Even parents, who love our children most tenderly, are not that intimately in tune with the smallest details of their lives.Don't ever let the enemy tell you that God has forgotten you. We are all sinful by nature, but our sins are not greater than His mercy. "The righteous cry out, and the Lord hears them." (Psa. 18: 3; 34: 17). And of course, we cry out to Him, *not our in own* righteousness, but that of the Lord Jesus, which is imputed to us. Because of that precious robe, we are assured that God hears our prayers. **Faith says what God says.**

Write Hebrews 6: 10 and speak it over your life.

†

When The Answer Is Delayed

"God has not forgotten you or turned His face from you," (Psa. 94: 14). He said He would never leave you or forsake you. He said, "Truly I am with you always."

You are His son or daughter, and that makes you blessed, but also a target for the powers of darkness.

If the answer to your prayer is a long time in coming, be of good courage while you wait on the Lord. Remember the angel Gabriel, who appeared to Daniel (Dan. 10: 12). He came *"because of Daniel's words."* The answer was on the way, but Gabriel was delayed for 21 days. He required the assistance of the archangel Michael before he got through to Daniel.

Ask the Lord to strengthen your heart (Psalm 27: 14). He has promised to do it. Even if He has to send an angel.

Do not doubt that God sends His angels. Write Luke 22: 43 and Heb. 1: 13-14.

Caution: Some people have strayed into error, thinking they can pray to angels. We do not pray angels. It is the Father Who directs the angels to their assignments (Psalm 91: 11). **Do Not Settle for Less**

Yes, I know, it's easy to get discouraged when you pray and do not see the answer on the way. Yes, I know that it's easier to accept the natural order of things rather than to take a stand for a supernatural answer from the Kingdom. It's easier to say, God has a reason and then do nothing rather than to resist the enemy with a good fight of faith.

I want to encourage you never to give up. We do not have to beg God to do what He has already done for us. We simply learn how to receive it.

As I read the ninth chapter of Acts, I am struck by four things. First Saul (later re-named Paul) was *not* seeking God like the Ethiopian eunuch was, but Saul did have a passion for righteousness. He mistakenly thought righteousness could be earned by keeping the Mosaic law and he was seriously intent on defending it. Second, Saul immediately acknowledged Jesus as **Lord** on the road to Damascus. Third while he was praying in verse 11, God knew exactly where Saul was, and gave instructions to Ananias to go there and restore his sight (God works through people). Fourth, Saul had to become blind to the natural world's light in order to see the Light of the world.

God knows exactly where you are and what you are praying for. He has the answer on the way. Do not be discouraged if it doesn't manifest for three days, or 21 days (Dan. 10:12) or even longer. **Faith says what God Says.**

Write Psalm 40: 11 and speak it in your daily prayers.

†

No Grace In Perfectionism

Hurrah and hallelujah! I can't make myself perfect. Why is that thought worth a glad "hurrah"?

Consider Moses' first miracle was turning water into blood (Ex 7:20). The first of Christ's miracles was turning water into wine at the wedding in Cana.

The six stone vessels at the wedding in Cana were used for ceremonial cleansing. They represent man's attempt to cleanse himself by rules and regulations. Jesus filled them with wine, a symbol of the new and better covenant.

There is no grace in perfectionism. Jesus replaces our efforts to cleanse ourselves with the new wine of the Holy Spirit, which brings joy, life, and *health to all our flesh* (Rom. 8: 11).

Hurrah! I'm free from legal perfectionism.

I receive His righteousness through faith and grace.

Example prayer:

Father, thank You for showing us that when Jesus turned the water into wine, a symbol of His blood and of the new covenant instituted at the Last Supper, it is also a type of the Holy Spirit. We are living stones (I Peter 2: 5), and like the stone vessels, I ask you to fill me with the new wine of Your Holy Spirit daily, that I may become a living temple,

strong and fit to do the works appointed to me from the foundation of the world (Eph. 2: 10). Amen. Hurrah. Hallelujah.

†

Feeling Weak? It's A Lie.

No matter how weak or ineffective you and I feel at times, we have POWER available to us. Ephesians 1:19-20 says, "How tremendous is the **power** *available* to us who believe in God. That power is the same divine power which was demonstrated in Christ when God raised Him from the dead."Our Great and Mighty God called the universe into existence and raised Jesus from the dead by His great power. He can handle any problem you are facing. If your own body is considered as dead as 90-year-old Sara's womb, it's no problem. God specializes in hopeless cases. You may say, "You don't know my finances" or "You don't know my health problems," or "You don't know my children's' problem." God knows, and He makes the power of His Word, which is the ultimate power, available to you. Get hold of His promises and *speak them to the problem* until it is removed and cast into the sea (Mark 11: 23-24).**Faith says what God says.**

Write Acts 1: 8 and Mark 11: 23-24 and speak them over your life.

Acting On Faith

I'm not delusional. I know there are things I cannot do. I can't be a gymnast for instance, even if I try to act like one.

I also know there are promises in God's word that are available only *when* I **ACT** by faith like they are true. Even when it seems they are *not manifesting*. Even when the enemy is hurling rocks at me, and I'm hurting. I have God's word on it that what I cannot do in my weakness is possible by the power of God (Matt. 19: 26).

I also know that the powerful prayers of believers can rescue me. The enemy tried to kill Paul when he was stoned to death at Lystra, but the *brothers prayed* over him. Paul got up and *walked* to Derbe the next day. No doubt his body was black and blue from the stoning.

When we are weak, God sends support and renews our strength. The hard knocks won't keep us down. The prayers of believers like Vickie Haller, Susie Lewis, Marla Woodmansee, Lisa Ham, and so many others who exercise their authority in Christ can speak life over dying hopes.

We can get up and walk, acting like God's word is true, even if we are beaten black and blue by the oppressor. Even when we look *delusional* to the rationale of others. Those people, who think we are off track, are simply walking by natural light. They cannot discern spiritual truths yet. **Faith says what God says.**

Write I Cor. 2: 14 and Matt. 19: 26. Do not let others convince you that healing is impossible or that you are crazy. Keep acting by faith in the Word.

†

Do You Know What A Powerful Weapon You Have?

You know the story. David defeats the giant and "*there was no sword in the hand of David*," I Sam. 17: 50.

However, young David had a powerful weapon, **"the sword of the spirit which is the Word of God" (Eph. 6:17).** He declared faith-filled words to the giant: "You come with a spear and a shield, but I come in the Name of the Lord, the God of the armies of Israel, whom you have defied. . . This day the Lord will deliver you into my hand, and I will take your head," (I Sam. 17: 45-47).

David spoke his faith and got what he said. He spoke like God speaks. He declared the end from the beginning. If you attend to God's Word, you have the same powerful sword of the Spirit in your heart and in your mouth (Rom. 10: 8). Use it like David did. Speak to the giant (sickness, financial woes, etc.) who defies the Word of God with his threats against you. Cut off his head with God's word. **Faith says what God says.**

Write out Psa. 34: 17-19. Speak these verses in your daily prayers.

†

Whose Image?

Jesus held up a Roman coin and asked whose image was on it. The crowd answered, "Caesar's." He then instructed, "Render unto Caesar the things that are Caesar's and unto God the things that are God's" (Luke 10: 25).

I read that verse often and thought it was all about taxes and tithes. Then the Spirit whispered, "In whose image are you made?" Why of course! We are being conformed to the image of the Lord (Rom. 8: 29). Oh, I see. I am to render unto God the things that are His. That includes myself. Conformed to His image. I am flesh becoming the Word.

Write Rom. 12: 1-2 below and do what it says.

†

Learning About Deliverance

The Bible does say, *"Many are the afflictions of the righteous"* (Psalm 34:19). However, this is only part of the truth. The rest of this scripture is, *"But the Lord delivers him out of them all."* People who blame God for *"afflictions"* have not learned the good part—deliverance!

Jesus said all things are possible to them that believe. If church is about only what we can accomplish in our human strength, then why would Jesus have had to come? He came to make inoperative the works of the devil *in our lives in this age.*

He taught us by example to do the same. When the devil had finished trying the Lord with every temptation, he departed from Jesus, waiting for a more opportune time, (Luke 4:13). The time Jesus spent in the wilderness was not the only attempt by Satan to derail him. Christ's defeat of the enemy in this scene was not final.

Throughout his ministry Jesus would confront Satan in many forms. Peter's misunderstanding of Jesus' calling, Peter's denial of Jesus, Judas' betrayal, and the ruling leaders' lies and accusations against Jesus, to name a few. Yet Jesus stood firm and true to his calling.

Satan will hurl his fiery darts towards us at any opportune time. At our moment of susceptibility and weakness. We are told in 1 Peter 5:8 that 'the enemy the devil prowls around like a roaring lion looking for someone to devour.' Lions attack sick, young or straggling animals. They choose victims who are alone or not alert.

That is why we need to fellowship with believers of like, precious faith.

Example prayer:

Father forgive me for asking You to do what Jesus said *I should do* in Matt. 10: 8. Resist. Overcome. Heal the sick. Cast out devils. Raise the dead. Freely give. Teach me to walk in this boldness, Lord. If I don't do it, who will? Sickness, death, and devils will defeat others who might have been set free. I pledge to You that I will not permit that to happen as long as I am operating in Your power and authority. Keep me also Lord, from willful sin. For I would not be a worker of iniquity, but of righteousness. Amen.

Testimony:

As a former psychic and satanic priest, Evangelist Tim Thompson has experienced deliverance from many afflictions in his body and soul. In his words:

"I have learned that seducing spirits are very real. Their main purpose is to drive you away from God's authority, His righteousness, and His people in every way possible with empty promises and lies. After I began to turn from evil spirits and seek the Truth, because I was dying, I had a visitation from Jesus. The doctor who had said my liver and kidneys were shutting down, re-tested them. 'This is impossible! Your body is healed,' he said. My doctors said they had never seen anything like it."

Tim Thompson's ministry today is to set the captives free from the torment of evil spirits (Isa. 61: 1). Jesus is all about that!

†

Who Is The Obedient Slave?

The most powerful Truth the Lord has shown me this week is found in Mark 5: 12: The devils begged Jesus to let them go into the herd of 2,000 swine.

When Jesus spoke, those devils *had to obey* His Word. It wasn't a man who obeyed His word. It was a legion of demons. They have to do what He says. We are no longer the slaves who must obey the lies of the devil. Instead, the devils have to **OBEY** *Christ in us* when we speak His words! However, if we do not submit first to God and then take authority over them and command them to leave, they will continue to steal the kingdom blessings from us. **Faith says what God says.**

Write James 4: 7-8. Speak it to the enemy. Example: I submit myself to my heavenly Father, the righteous Judge of all the earth and confess I am His child. I draw near to Him with worship and praise. I resist you Satan. You have to flee from me in the Name of Jesus. Praise God, I'm free from your oppression. Amen.

How Will You Believe
The Heavenly Things?

Jesus says in John 3:12, "If I have told you earthly things and you do not believe, how will you believe if I tell you heavenly things?"

Jesus asks how will you believe heavenly things?

Doubt robs us of the boldness to do great and mighty things by Christ's heavenly power in us. Doubt that His authority in the believer is enough to do what He said to do in Matthew 10: 8, "Heal the sick, raise the dead, cure the lepers, cast out demons and set the captives free."

Write Gen. 21: 6 here. Who shares in the joyous laughter of Sarah's supernatural birth?

Example prayer:

Father, forgive me when doubt based on other people's experience, or based on my own experiences, robs me of the boldness I need. Abraham had no precedent at all to believe God would make him a father of many nations. He and Sarah had never seen a 90-yr.-old woman give birth. He had nothing but Your word. Today we have a more sure word in Jesus. I make a demand on the seed of faith in my spirit to grow and produce a harvest to the glory of your name. Amen.

Faith Says What God Says by Harriett Ford

†

When Death Threatens

Sometimes God allows the serpent to bite.

In Acts 28: 5, a viper fastened onto Paul's arm. He simply shook off the deadly snake into the fire. We can do the same. Tell that old serpent that the fire is where he is headed. Jesus gave His followers power to tread on serpents, scorpions and over all the power of the enemy.

I am convinced that Satan can't harm us until we are satisfied (Psa. 91: 16) and have completed our assignments. If he threatens you with death, tell that old serpent, "I'll be in a far better place, but I'm not leaving here until I finish the task the Lord has given me." Then shake him off.

When the people saw that Paul did not die, the obvious miracle caused them to realize God was at work.

Fear is to Satan what faith is to God. Both will manifest. Faith calls forth the evidence of God at work in your life. Fear brings forth the evidence of Satan at work in your life.

Write Num. 14: 9. Note: the evil report caused fear and rebellion. Who told them that God would abandon them? What happens when we fail to act on God's promised Word?

No Cure? No Hope?

Do you have an illness for which the doctors say has no cure? Who told you that it's impossible to be healed?

You know there are promises of healing in God's word. Have you read the promises and tried to increase your faith, but the symptoms remain?

I've heard it said that some people are waiting for a *rhema* word spoken directly from God. A word of knowledge that is specifically spoken over them to confirm that they can believe God for their healing to manifest.

They want a phone call from heaven, when God has already sent letters filled with promises. They want that word which Jesus spoke to the centurion, who asked Him to "**speak the word only and he shall be healed**."

Guess what. God has already spoken it in Psalm 107:20. "He sends His word and heals them; He delivers them from their graves." His words are spirit, life, and health to all your flesh.

Here is a simple way to get a rhema word from the Lord. Take the "logos" (James 1:22) and act on it. When you are doers of the Word, the logos (written word) becomes rhema (living word). **Faith says what God says.**

Faith Says What God Says by Harriett Ford

Example prayer:

Father, I am speaking Your words back to You: Psalm 30:2-3, "Oh Lord my God, I cried to You and You have healed me. You have brought up my soul from the grave." Psalm 49:15, You redeem my soul from the power of the grave. Psalm 103: 1-4, You are the Lord Who redeems me and heals all my diseases. You are the One Who said all things are possible to them that believe. I will not let the enemy tell me this isn't working. There is NOTHING more powerful than God's word. Amen

†

Sozo, Yashi, Yeshua

Psalm 145:18-19 says, "The Lord is near to all who call on him, to all who call on him in truth. He fulfills the desire of those who fear him; he also hears their cry and **saves** them."

The word "saves" in scripture has a much greater meaning than I first realized. It is always a present tense (on-going) verb, not just a one-time event as in "saved" when I accepted Jesus as my Lord.

According to the Hebrew meaning, *save* is the word *Yashi* and means "deliverance, aid, victory, prosperity, health, help, salvation, and welfare."

The Greek word for *save* is *Sozo*, which means "to save, deliver, protect, heal, preserve, do well, and be made whole."

Jesus' work of salvation is ongoing in the life of a believer. He promises He will not cease till it is perfected (Phil. 1: 6). The Hebrew meaning for our Savior's name, Yeshua, (Jesus) is "to save, rescue, preserve, and get victory" on an ongoing basis.

Example prayer:

Father I thank You that every time I say the name of Jesus, I am proclaiming complete victory in my earthly life. I am delivered from the evil one, protected, healed, rescued and victorious. Do I look

like it at all times? Not always. Neither did Paul look totally victorious after his many beatings, shipwrecks, and even a stoning. But my faith is the evidence of things unseen. You hear my prayer and I am saved. Praise the Lord. Amen.

†

I Was Astonished

"The Name of the Lord is a strong tower; the righteous run into it and are saved," Prov. 18: 10. I grew up singing worship songs such as *His Name is Wonderful* and *There's Power in the Blood*. These words took on a startling and powerful new meaning one night when an evil spirit visited my room. Until that moment, I had never realized how real the kingdom of darkness is. I was too intellectual, too college educated to believe that evil spirits actually exist and are active in this present world. The devil and his minions were not part of my belief system. However, my spirit had been born again into the Kingdom of Light (Col. 1: 13) which is filled with angelic spirits. The evil rulers in the kingdom of darkness are also angelic beings (Rev. 12: 9). They are just as real.

When I became aware of the evil spirit in my room, my heart began pounding. Before fear could take a paralyzing hold on me, I heard the Holy Spirit whisper, "All who call on the **Name** of the Lord shall be saved." Immediately I shouted out with all my might, "Jesus!"

At once, the demon disappeared, banished by the Name above all names. I had run into the Name of the Lord and I was protected. My heart stopped pounding, and my mind marveled. I had always understood that verse in Romans 10: 13 to mean that once I confessed my sins to Jesus and called Him my Lord, I was "saved." It was settled at that moment. I didn't realize that calling on the Name of the Lord has much greater significance. Salvation is an ongoing experience. His Name is our *daily* PROTECTION from the evil one (John 17: 15). **Faith says what God says.**

Write John 17: 12.

Example prayer:

Heavenly Father, You protected Jesus' followers by the *POWER of Your Name* (John 17:12). Lord Jesus, You asked the Father to protect all believers in that *Name.* So, when I call out, "Jesus!" I have all the *power* of Your name to deliver me from evil. In the Name of Jesus, I take authority over the enemy. He has to flee from me and take his attack with him (Acts 10: 38). Praise God.

Both Covenants Include Healing

"I AM the Lord who heals you," (Ex. 15: 26). God did not say, "I WAS the Lord who heals you."

The laughable story is told of a woman who heard the doctor say he had done all he could and now she must pray. She answered, "You mean it's come to that!?" She had been taught that supernatural healing has passed away from the church.

People who have been taught wrongly, or who have had an unfortunate experience, often turn their back on the 'healing gospel.' I did that too at one time—turned off the TV preachers who taught faith and stopped praying for the sick. However, the Holy Spirit began to lead me where I had once refused to go.

A careful student of the Law of the Spirit of Life in Christ Jesus (Rom. 8) learns that healing is just as available today as when Jesus walked the earth. Jesus Himself said healing is the children's bread (Matt. 15: 26).

God would have to violate His word if today He took back healing *from both* the Old Mosaic Covenant and the new and better covenant (Heb. 8: 6) which Jesus paid for with His perfect blood.

He expected Covenant people to come to Him for healing (2 Chron. 16: 12). He was displeased when King Asa went to the physicians for healing instead of to Him.

When the Hebrews put the lamb's blood on the doors of their homes, the angel of death had to pass over them. They came out of Egypt and there not one sick or feeble among them (Psalm 105: 37). Over half a million people strong and healthy! That is a miracle in itself. In a church, you can find very few people who don't have a single physical complaint today.

There is POWER in the blood. The lamb's blood in Exodus symbolized the blood of the Perfect Lamb of God Who comes to redeem us. The actual Savior's New-Covenant blood is certainly not less powerful than the blood of a lamb born in Egypt. **Faith says what God says.**

Write Heb. 8: 6-7 and ask for revelation of what is included in the New Covenant.

Eating Without Discernment

Christians have pointed to the verses in I Cor. 11: 29 regarding judgment for believers who "disrespect" the Lord's supper.

I believe the problem was not disrespect. It was the believers who did not discern the blood of the Lamb. "For he that eateth and drinketh unworthily, eateth and drinketh damnation to himself, not discerning the Lord's body." For if you do not recognize the meaning of the Lord's body when you eat the bread and drink from the cup, you permit judgment on yourself as you eat and drink.

First Cor 11:30 says, "For this cause many are weak and sickly among you." God says His people perish for lack of knowledge, according to Hosea 4: 6. He sent His word, His Son's blood, His provision for divine health. It is up to us to access it. Remember in Egypt, the angel of death had to pass over the blood on the doorposts and lintels of the house. And there was **"not one sick or feeble among the Hebrews,"** when they left Egypt the next day (Psalm 105: 37).

If church-goers are never taught this powerful truth about the physical blessings purchased by the blood of the Lamb, they do fall sick and many die because of a lack of *discernment.* They must learn to discern how powerful the blood of Jesus is and how it brings healing not only to the spirit, but to the soul and body as well. I have read numerous testimonies about people who received healing through eating the bread and drinking the cup in honor of the Lord's sacrifice.

Write Exodus 12: 13 and Psa. 105: 37. Speak these verses over your life.

†

What Is Meant By *Destruction of the Flesh*?

Destruction of the flesh? Let's look at how this term is used in the New Testament.

In I Corinthians 5: 5, Paul said to turn a man over to Satan for the destruction of the flesh so that his spirit might be saved. In his second letter (2 Cor. 2: 7-8) Paul says that same man should be restored gently so that he would not be overwhelmed by excessive sorrow. Obviously, his flesh was not destroyed.

A better interpretation is that his lust of the flesh was what needed destroying. What then, is the meaning of that ambiguous phrase, "for the destruction of the flesh"? The sense almost certainly is this: Turn the man over to Satan (i.e., back into the world community) that he may reap the consequences of his rebellion. Remove him from a warm, loving association with his church family. Under such circumstances, if he had a remnant of conscience remaining, the rogue brother might well learn to "destroy" his baser, "fleshly" urges, and then be restored to live for the Savior's purpose.

It is the LOVE of God that leads us to repentance (Rom. 2: 4). Not His scourging wrath.

†

Why Do We Need Keys?

A key is for unlocking something. Usually a door or a cabinet or even a treasure chest. Jesus gave Peter the keys to the Kingdom. What do they unlock? Why must we have a key to unlock what Jesus died to give us? And think about this. Do keys also lock someone out? What are the keys and how do we use them? The Bible uses a key as a symbol of authority. In Isaiah 22:22, we see Eliakim the priest receiving "the key of the house of David…on his shoulder." A trusted servant to the king wore the key to the king's house on a hook on his shoulder. Therefore, he had the authority to open or close the king's house. Revelation 3:7 speaks of Jesus having the key of King David. In ancient Israel, the human king was in fact the steward of God, the true King of the land. Similarly, the divine Christ is the steward of His Father's Kingdom. In Luke 10: 19, Jesus gave authority to His followers. In Luke 11: 52, Jesus says knowledge is the key to the kingdom. We also have the key of authority. We exercise it by the power of the tongue. Daily.

Has the enemy tried to steal God's promises from you? Cast down doubt, fear, and anything that exalts itself against the truth of God's word in the Name of Jesus. You may feel like you are talking to the air, but remember, Satan and his angels dwell in the "power of the air" (Eph. 2: 2). They hear and respond to the Word of God. All angels do.

Write 2 Cor. 10: 5 and Dan. 10: 12 here.

Testimony:

I have seen the Lord do what I call a chiropractic adjustment on spinal columns many times in response to the prayer of authority. In fact, I have *never* seen a time when I held a person's heels in my hands that God did not immediately adjust them to equal length (except once for a man with a crippling injury). Praise God.

When I visited Anita and Tim Koch at their home in North Carolina, I saw that she was in need. Below is her message to me after prayer:

Harriett,

I just had to write to tell you a marvelous praise report! Your prayer over me for the straightening of my spine truly caused a miraculous result! Tim and I, still in South Florida (now Boca Raton at our sister-in-law's), went to see our long-time chiropractor yesterday for a "tune up", which we do every year when we're here. For the first time ever, over the many years—30 or so—he has treated us (me through several car accidents), he said my heels are totally aligned! I have always had one hip higher than the other, but now, no more! I'm in super good shape!

I thought you would be delighted to hear this. And I don't even remember what you did besides pray over me! Tim asked if you anointed me with oil, but I don't remember. You obviously have the gift of healing, as we all can set in motion. We have anointed and prayed over many of our guests when the Spirit so moved us to, but in this case it was immediate!

Thank you, Harriett, and give our love to John.

Anita, Lake Lure, North Carolina

Testimony:

At a recent book-signing event, my attention was drawn to a woman clearly in pain. She said she had suffered severe injuries from an accident. When I asked if she wanted prayer, she said yes. I knelt and took her feet in my hands. Seeing one leg was at least an inch shorter than the other, I thanked God for lengthening the short one. Slowly the legs adjusted until they were equal. The woman smiled and walked away. Later, she returned to say all her hip pain had vanished. Praise God.

The Sword Must Be Spoken

Does God hear unspoken prayers from our heart? Of course He does (Jn. 11: 42). Praise and thanksgiving are from the heart and often turn into songs. However, the sword of the spirit is the Word of God given to defeat the enemy. It is a weapon of warfare, and I have come to believe it does not become a sword until it is **spoken** from the mouth out of a heart of faith. Consider how we are instructed to use the sword of the Spirit: "Let the redeemed of the Lord *say* so." Psalm 107. "Let the weak *say* I am strong," (Joel 3: 10). "I will *say* of the Lord, He is my refuge and my fortress," (Psalm 91: 2). Believers *speak* a language of faith based on God's word. No word, no faith. God is a rewarder of them that diligently seek Him. No seeking, no reward. He said to resist the devil and he will flee. No resisting, no enemy fleeing. No *speaking* authority, no victory. A warrior fills up his spirit with God's Word every day. He takes the sword of the spirit and *speaks* to the mountain, the sycamore tree, the body which is not in line with the word. Then having done all, he stands therefore (Eph. 6: 13) with patience in the hope of His coming—coming with every answer to every word-based prayer *spoken* from a heart of faith. I didn't say that. God did.

Write 2 Cor. 1: 20. What has God said to you that you are having difficulty believing?

†

Bondage Is Not From God

Two thousand years ago, Jesus' ministry was to set free "all whom Satan had bound" (Luke 13:10-16) and to heal ". . . all that were oppressed of the devil."(Acts 10:38) And that is STILL His ministry today.

In John 10: 10, Jesus tells us that Satan (not God) is the thief who comes to steal, kill, and destroy. Bondage is authored by Satan. This is not the way God intends for man to live, although there are those who teach that God uses illness, bondage, and suffering to teach us patience. Any pastor knows that he has plenty of people in his congregation who can teach him patience (Numbers 33: 55).

This is a reminder. A careful study of the New Testament and especially of Paul's struggles clearly reveal it is *persecution* for the Word's sake which all believers will face (Mark 4: 17; 2 Tim. 3:12). God doesn't stop people from hating and persecuting believers. Why? because He honors free will.

Look at Matthew 24:14. and Luke 9:2. The apostles are sent to proclaim good news of the kingdom of God and to **heal.** I used to think the good-news message was all about repentance so that when we die, we can go to Heaven. It is NOT just that. The kingdom of God is invading earth now, equipping believers to overcome the works of the devil (sickness, oppression, bondage, depression, etc.) But overcoming is NOT automatic. We must learn to walk in victory by exercising our God-given authority.

Write Luke 10: 19-20 and speak it over your life. Note: the believer's authority is over *spirits* who want to oppress and put people in bondage.

†

Prayers Of Darkened Understanding?

Before I knew God's Word is God's will I prayed out of a darkened understanding. I was sincere, but not well informed. Therefore, I was praying amiss. The Holy Spirit made intercession for me (Rom. 8: 26).

God always hears the cry of a seeking heart, no matter how uninformed we are.

Jesus knows what people are thinking in their hearts according to Luke 5: 22; Mark 2: 8; and Matt. 9:4. However, He expects us to study and to grow in our faith, as newborn babes desiring the sincere milk of the Word (II Tim. 2: 15).

As I grew in knowledge of the scriptures, I found that when I was praying God's Word back to Him, I was assured of the answer. I also learned this does not always happen suddenly. I have looked many years for answers to some of my prayers, which I know are according to His will. I believe the answers are mine and are coming to pass. That is what patience is for (Heb. 10:36).

Write Psalm 34: 15 and I John 5: 14-15.

†

Lock Out The Thief

Jesus drove the money changers out of the Temple saying, "You have made it a den of thieves," (Matt. 21: 13).

There has been no temple in Jerusalem since the Romans destroyed it in 70 A.D. However there still remains a temple for worship. "Don't you know your body is the temple of the Holy Ghost, which is in you?" (I Cor. 6: 15-20).

Jesus also gave believers the keys of the Kingdom, not just for entering into the spiritual kingdom on earth, but for resisting the works of the devil, (John 10: 10).

You already know that keys unlock Kingdom blessings on earth as in heaven, (Deut. 11: 21). They also are for locking out the works of the thief. Drive out the den of thieves who are trying to steal your blood-bought blessings. Then lock the door of your heart. Here is how you do that: **Faith says what God says.**

Write Psalm 101: 3 and Prv. 4: 23.

The God Of Now

We live in a linear, three-dimensional time here on earth: past, present, and future. God, Who is the Great AM, lives outside of those limits. He is a continual presence. As I read how Jesus raised Lazarus from the dead, I'm struck by the words He used. Martha was saying, "I know my brother will rise again at the resurrection." She expected it in the future.

Jesus answered, "I AM the resurrection and the life." He used the present tense verb, AM. He did not say, I WILL be the resurrection in the future, although that is how we understand the word most often, and it is not a wrong understanding. However, Jesus proceeded to demonstrate His power over death by calling Lazarus forth right then and there to demonstrate His word.

Those who are acquainted with accounts of believers who have called forth the dead, (Smith Wigglesworth, Andrew Wommack, Brenda Lange and many others) understand that Jesus' entire ministry was to reverse the curse of the law of sin AND DEATH by ushering in a new and better covenant, the Law of the Spirit of Life (Rom. 8: 2).

You say, well that was Jesus. Yes, and He still IS the great I AM, who was and IS and IS to come (notice the Bible's use of present tense verbs). He is the resurrection and the life. My Hebrew translation of the Bible calls God The Always Present One. He will never leave you nor forsake you. He is with you always, and it is always now where He is.

Write 2 Cor. 6: 2.

Example prayer:

Heavenly Father, I see that Jesus is the Resurrection and the life, not the Destruction and the Death. Today is the day of salvation. Not tomorrow. I say that I receive Your salvation, Sozo, deliverance, and renewal daily by faith in Your Word. Amen.

†

What We Cannot Do

"She has done what she could," said Jesus of the woman who "anointed his body for burial ahead of time," Mark 14:8.

The woman recognized what she could not do for herself—atone for her sins. She did what she could. The most important thing anyone could do. She worshiped Jesus. She gave an offering of expensive perfume. Perhaps a gift from a former lover. Perhaps her entire income for the year ahead, signifying that her life was forever changed. She gave her all.

She didn't know then that shortly after she poured the perfume over Him, Jesus would become the *sweet-smelling* sacrificial Lamb of God and that she had done this for his burial. She only knew that He had forgiven her much, and she loved him with total devotion.

I ask myself, have I done what I could? Do I need to give more money? Pray longer? Read more chapters in the Bible each day? Increase my giving?

And I seem to hear the voice of my gentle shepherd. "I do not need all your money. I own the cattle on a thousand hills. I want to spend time with you."

Write Lev. 1: 9 and Eph. 5: 2 and make those verses into a prayer.

Faith Says What God Says by Harriett Ford

Example prayer:

Lord, how wonderful you are. Worthy of my total devotion. I want to do all that I can to be in Your presence. For only in Your presence is fullness of joy, unspeakable and full of glory. The First and most important thing I can do is to acknowledge Jesus as my Lord and Savior and praise Him no matter what is happening in my life, bad or good. In that way, "We are to God the sweet aroma of Christ among those who are being saved . . ." (2 Cor. 2: 15). Thank You Jesus. Amen.

†

From The Wicked One

Proverbs 3:25 says, "Do not be afraid of sudden terror, nor of trouble from the *wicked* when it comes." The sudden terror or trouble comes from where? From the wicked. Say it again. From the wicked. Sudden terror, tribulation and affliction comes from the wicked. Of course. That's why Jesus taught us to pray, *deliver us from the evil one.*

Readers are seeing this same message throughout this book. It bears repeating because of hardened hearts and those having difficulty with false teaching. Pastor Jack Hayford says: "Let's get this right. From Jesus' own lips we have the strategy of the wicked one walking about seeking whom he may devour. In John the tenth chapter, verse ten, Jesus describes His people as sheep and He is the Shepherd. He says it is the thief who comes to steal, kill or destroy the sheep. Satan comes to steal seeds of faith. He is out to destroy, to break down, to ruin health, take away resources, devastate your situation, break down your emotions, confuse your mind, bring hopelessness."

Now contrast that with Jesus. He has come to bring life and that more abundant. This does not happen automatically just because we are Christians. We have weapons of warfare that will make the devil flee from us. We learn the law meditation which unlocks the blessings and benefits of Proverbs 4: 22. "My son, let them (God's word) not depart from your eyes; keep them in the midst of your heart. For they are LIFE to those who find them and health to all your *flesh*."

We look to the Eternal, Mighty, Powerful, Unchanging God. Get our eyes on Him and speak faith-language. Lord, I come to you for your wisdom to show me what to do in this situation and bring You glory.

Testimony:

Overcoming death by the language of faith. In August of 2013, a woman named Arlene was given three to six months to live. She had gone from weighing 137 to a pitiful 103 Lbs. and was down to a size 00. By grace she believed Proverbs 4: 20-27 and put those words into practice. Arlene says, "I started reading the 100 healing scriptures aloud every day for three years.

Three years later, in November of 2016, my blood cells are completely healed and functioning. I weigh 122 Lbs. and wear size four. No medication. Word only!

God cannot lie.
(www.hopefaithprayer.com/scriptures/100-god-healing-david-emigh/)

Testimony:

I parked in my usual space at work that day. At least three times, I pulled out again and my attention was drawn to the car parked alongside the wall behind me instead of in a diagonal space. At one point I actually said aloud, *I will not back into that car.*

That afternoon as I was leaving work, my boss walked me out to the car as he always does. Mindful of the rough neighborhood, he "rides shotgun" with all his employees to see them safely off. This time he was speaking to me about my excellent efforts that day. Watching him wave as he walked away, I backed too far and my car struck the one parked parallel to the building behind me.

As I pondered this frustrating accident, I was tempted to ask, "Lord why didn't you stop me?" The Lord impressed on me that He *had* pointed out that vehicle to me three times that day, and I had spoken aloud that I would not back into it. I simply did not heed the warning.

That led me to think about how many accidents and other bad things could have been avoided if we only heed God's warning.

Sometimes our receivers are simply not picking up the message. Can we blame God for that?

Write Joshua 1: 8. How does success come?

†

When God Makes You Wait

The Lord spoke to my heart that one reason people do not receive an instant healing is because they are not deeply rooted and grounded in the Word. If God healed them instantly, the fowls of the air could easily steal the healing from them.

Let's read Mark 4: 15-18. Some people are like seed along the path, where the word is thrown. As soon as they hear it, Satan comes and takes away the word that was sown in them. Others are like the people on rocky places. They hear the word and at once receive it with joy. **Mark 4: 17:** <u>But they themselves have no root, and they remain for only season. When trouble or persecution comes because of the word, they quickly fall away.</u>

A seed, once planted in good soil takes time to grow. You don't get an instant harvest overnight. Mark 4: 28 said the earth produces first the blade, then the ear, then the full corn in the ear.

Joyce Meyer defines an instant healing as a "suddenly." We also have healings that are defined as "recovery," which is a process of return to a normal state of health, mind, or strength. This can be both a natural or a supernatural process, as in the recovery from what doctors have diagnosed as in incurable disease.

Jesus said His followers, both yesterday and today, will lay hands on the sick and <u>they shall **recover**,</u> Matt 16: 17-18.

In other words, the sick do not always get an instant healing. That does not mean they don't have faith. Abraham, the father of faith, had to wait until he was 100 years old for the promised child to be born. So, while we are recovering, what do we do? Don't allow your waiting period to make you hopeless. Maybe there is nothing physically happening that your eyes can see but there is definitely something happening in the spiritual realm as you learn to rely on Christ.

Write Psalm 27: 14.

Example prayer:

Father I will not give up. I will keep on keeping on like Abraham did, agreeing with the Word of God. I will keep my mind fixed on what is above, and not on what I see in the natural. I establish in my heart the promise in God's word that I am waiting to receive. God's Word is the incorruptible seed. It cannot fail to produce a harvest that is rooted in good soil. Praise God. Amen.

Is There Ever A Time To Give Up?

Quit believing for a miracle? Just accept what the thief has stolen from you and live in defeat? Remember Jonah. He didn't give up. Remember Abraham, Zechariah, and Hannah? They waited for years and years and didn't give up. Remember Effell Bar Effell. No? That's because he's the one who gave up.

Maintaining Is A Must! Everything requires maintaining. Your house, your car, your pets, your body. *Your faith.* I know personally of people who received divine healing and later lost it. They did not have their faith deeply rooted and grounded in the Word of God (Matt. 13: 5). When the enemy came again with lying symptoms, they accepted them and assumed they had not actually received healing after all. They did not know how to maintain their confidence.

Hebrews 10: 35-37 says to cast not away your confidence, which promises great reward. They did not know how to say, "Body you have already been healed and you have to come in line with the word of God. I command these symptoms to leave in Jesus' Name. Jesus is Lord over disease. Disease does not lord it over me." They did not know how stand firmly on the solid rock of the word until the storm passed.

Yes, there is a good fight of faith when sickness tries to return. But this is a battle that is already won in the spiritual kingdom. Faith will bring healing into the natural realm. Faith that has been maintained by continuing in the words of God, speaking those words, and resisting the enemy. Maintenance requires looking beyond the natural, renewing the mind to the supernatural, which is simply the principle of walking not by sight, but by faith. You can win the fight by continuing in the Word (John 8: 31).

Example prayer:

Father, I continue to speak your healing words, planting them in my spirit and soul, and I refuse to cast my confidence away, even if I get a bad report. Your words are spirit, life, and health to all my flesh. These lying symptoms are defeated. I speak life and health to my body in Jesus' name. Amen.

Is It Sin To Blame God?

A careful look at the book of Job reveals that it is clearly NOT God who afflicts. It is the adversary walking about as a roaring lion seeking whom he may devour (Job 2: 2; 1 Pet. 5: 8).

The Lord showed me an example about blame. I permitted my 16-year-old daughter to drive a car. She ran a traffic light, got into an accident, and suffered a broken leg. Shards of glass are still embedded in her forehead years later. This was not my will. I did not cause it. Yet because I permitted her to drive, someone could ultimately blame me for the accident.

God permits. He does not cause. Satan has a plan to deceive people into thinking God is to blame for all troubles, either as a form of correcting, or by not intervening to stop the bad things from happening.

Job 1: 22 states, "Job did not sin against God by *blaming* Him" for the devastation in his life. This verse shows that it IS sin to blame God for troubles.

I know what you're thinking. Satan had to get permission from God to torment Job. True, but it *was NOT God* who did the tormenting. Job would have been guilty of sin if he blamed God. Torment, death and destruction are never God's will. He permits what people permit because He gave dominion to man. He had confidence in His servant Job, and simply removed the hedge around him (Job 1: 10). His perfect will is always to bless. After all, He sent His Son that we might have life abundant, not death and destruction (John 10: 10).

When Mrs. Job said, "You might as well curse God and die," she was agreeing with the devil instead of trusting in the goodness of God. That was Satan's objective. He wanted Job to *blame* God for his suffering and curse God to His face (Job 1: 11). The entire book of Job attempts to answer the why-bad-things-happen-to-good-people question. The three friends of Job bring up every possible, reasonable, and religious explanation. However, all their answers were incorrect. Man's attempt to explain God usually fails. Write Jeremiah 29: 11 and rejoice!

Example prayer:

Father, when we do not understand suffering, help us always to acknowledge that You are Love and Your plans toward us are to do us good and not harm. You love to give Your children good things. Thank You Father, that you provided through Jesus an inheritance of blessing in the land of the living. Amen.

Testimony:

I heard about a father who kept bringing a crippled child to the healing services. The boy did not get healed. Later when the evangelist puzzled about it, the Lord impressed on his heart: "This man was not seeking me. He only wanted healing for his son." The minister realized the boy's father was in need of healing for his own soul and was *refusing it.*

The man was seeking the gift but not the Giver.

What if he had been willing to give his heart to the Lord? Jeremiah wrote in Chapter 32: 39-41: "I will give them one heart and one way, that they may fear me forever, for their own good and the good of their children after them. . . I will rejoice in doing them good."

God wants to heal our hearts as well as our bodies, and our choices do have impact on our children.

Write Deut. 29: 29. What things of God have been revealed to you most recently?

Example prayer:

I will not question why some people do not receive kingdom blessings. I choose to receive the things that are revealed in Jesus—life more abundant, love peace and joy in the Holy Spirit. I choose to seek the Lord first with all my heart, not just for what He can do for me, but for Who He is. I choose this also for the good of my children after me. Amen.

†

Man's Attempt To Explain Suffering

The LORD said to Eliphaz the Temanite, "My wrath is kindled against you, and against your two friends: for ye have not spoken of me the thing that is right, as my servant Job has (Job 42:7).

What did they speak that was not right? Here is a great revelation. They blamed everything *but Satan* for Job's suffering.

Satan's plan all along was to manipulate Job into blaming God for his troubles. As before stated, when Mrs. Job said, "You might as well curse God and die," she was in full agreement with the devil's plot to get Job to curse God to His face (Job: 2: 4).

Yes, Satan had permission, but scriptures show plainly that it is Satan who does the afflicting. "Satan went from the presence of the Lord and struck Job with painful boils, (Job 2: 7).

God is not interested in doing us harm. Jeremiah 29: 11 says God plans to do His people "good and not harm." **Faith says what God says.**

Write I Thess. 5: 9.

Example prayer:

Father, I thank You that Your plans are to do me good and not harm. Forgive me for blaming the bad

things that happen on everything but what they should be attributed to. Thank You for restoring to Job his health and all that he lost. Thank You for restoring my health. You said Jesus came to make inoperative the works of the devil and that includes oppression, sickness, and disease. All praise, glory, honor, and thanksgiving be unto You forever. Amen.

How Can Both Be True?

An auto-antonym is a word with multiple meanings of which one is the reverse of another. For example, the word cleave can mean "to cut apart" or "to bind together." Some difficult doctrines in the Bible may be viewed in that category. The unsearchable riches of the incomparable wisdom of God are described in the Apostle Paul's words, "His ways are past finding out." How can two apparent contradictions both be true? And yet they simply are. God has two first born sons. He names Israel His "firstborn son" called out of Egypt in Ex. 4: 22. In the New Testament it's Jesus. "For those whom he foreknew he also predestined to be conformed to the image of his Son, in order that he might be the firstborn among many brothers. (Romans 8:29). Jesus, one hundred percent man and one hundred percent God. (He laid aside His divinity (Phil. 2: 7) and operated as a man with the same body of flesh as Adam's (I Cor. 15: 45-49). He was able to perform miracles under the anointing of the Holy Spirit which He sent to all believers. Good news! You must lose your life in order to save it. You must give in order to receive. When you are weak, then you are strong. You are chosen by God, but you also must choose Him. You must be blind in order to see best (walking by faith and not by sight). Jesus is the Lion of Judah. He is also the Lamb of God. What could be more opposite? Whoever would be great among you must be a servant. We must grow and mature in our faith and yet become as little children. Our sins are forgiven past, present and future, but continuing a life of sin can cause spiritual death (Matt. 7:21-23).

The grace of God has appeared to every man (Titus 2: 11), yet we know that few will find the path to life. There are names which were NOT written in the Book of Life from before the foundation of the world, (Rev. 17: 8) and yet Peter says it is NOT God's will that any should perish and that all would come to repentance. How can this be? How can both be true at the same time?

If we could explain it and have perfect understanding, we wouldn't be living by faith. We trust in the goodness, the faithfulness and the mercy of our all mighty God. His ways are past finding out. Yet Jesus tells us to seek, knock, and ask, and we shall find.

†

The Power Of Fasting

In the Bible, people often set apart a designated time of going without food in order to humble themselves and entreat the Lord's blessing or protection. My first experience with fasting was when I had been desperately praying for a child.

The words, "Why don't you fast?" kept whispering in my mind. I began to wonder if I was hearing the voice of the Holy Spirit. I decided to set apart three days to go without eating and bring my petition to the Lord.

The first day, I came home from my teaching my classes, and I was hungry. I opened the fridge and there were all my favorite foods. "Is this really the voice of the Holy Spirit telling me to fast, or just my own imagination?" I asked. My stomach growled. I decided to ask for a confirmation. Picking up my enormous, encyclopedic-style study Bible, I said, "Lord, If You really want me to fast, please show me a verse on fasting." I was fairly sure I would get to eat. Then I let the pages fall open. The first verse my eyes fell on read, "And they sanctified a fast unto the Lord."Wow. I thought of Gideon and how he had prayed a second time for confirmation of his assignment (Judges 6: 36-40). So, I asked the Lord a second time and let the pages fall open once more. Again, the first verse my eyes fell on was about fasting.

You'd think I would have gotten the message, but I dared to ask once more, ruling out any possibility of coincidence. The third time my huge book flopped open to verse on fasting. What are the odds? I went to bed hungry that night, but secure in the knowledge that God had directed me to this fast.

The second day, I had such a powerful and overwhelming experience with God. His presence enveloped me in a cloud of glorious joy, unspeakable and full of glory. I raised my hands toward heaven and said, "God if I never have a child that's okay. You are all I want and all I need in this world." You already know the answer. Nine months later I became the mother of a beautiful baby girl. Reading about Hannah in First Kings, chapter one, I recently realized she had the same experience. She *refused to eat her food* and went instead to the Tabernacle where she prayed earnestly for a child. God answered her prayer and gave her a baby boy, Samuel, the prophet who grew up to anoint the first two kings of Israel. The power of fasting can bring a breakthrough. However, the Lord impresses it on my mind that it is not a tool, to persuade God to change His mind. It is a weapon of warfare that pulls down strongholds in our lives (2 Cor. 10: 3-4).

Father, I thank You that when I laid the deepest desire of my heart on the altar of prayer as a sacrifice, You gave it back again. You made me a joyful mother of two precious daughters. All praise, honor, glory, splendor, majesty and thanksgiving be Yours forever. Amen.

†

The Word IS Jesus.

You may not get this the first time you read it. Or even the second or thirty-second time. There is something supernatural about the Word of God written in the pages of your Bible. Duh, you say every believer knows that. Do you know that the Word IS Jesus?

In the beginning was the Word, the Word was with God, and the Word WAS God. The Word IS a person. He became flesh and dwelt among us.

The written word of God is able to do everything that Jesus did. It is powerful, sharper than a two-edged sword, a discerner of the intents of the heart. It is Spirit and life and also health to all your flesh.

The Word is capable of reproducing life in the spirit of man, renewing his mind, and also healing his body. The washing and regeneration of the Word (Titus 3: 5) speaks of more than the rebirth of the spirit.

When a believer continues in the Word, reading, meditating, seeking, He is actually spending time with Jesus, learning what the Lord directs, becoming His disciple, and ALSO regenerating his own flesh.

Regeneration is defined as 1: an act or the process of regenerating: the state of being regenerated. 2: spiritual renewal or revival. 3: renewal or restoration of a body, bodily part, or biological system (such as a forest) after injury or as a normal process.

Wait a minute, you say. Just reading God's Word can

regenerate my mind, my spirit and also my body? I didn't say that. God did in Proverbs 4: 22 and many more scriptures as well. Find the verses for yourself. Seek *first* your relationship with Jesus, His kingdom, His righteousness, and He promises to add everything you need.

Write John 8: 31-32 and make a commitment to DO what it says. What sets you free?

†

Light Overcomes Darkness

You know the old saying: it's always darkest just before the dawn.

As often happens when I wake in the morning, the Lord lays a word on my heart for those who are in a dark place, perhaps discouraged and doubtful. When the answer they have been hoping for seems to be a long time in coming.

Satan wants you to question God's word. Readers know that his greatest ploy is to get you to ask, "Has God said?" Remember, Jesus IS the Word made flesh. He IS the Word which the Father sent to heal all disease and to overcome sin and the grave (Psalm 107: 20). He IS the resurrection.

Satan always tries to steal the Word and destroy the harvest (Mark 4: 14). When it looks like the kingdom of darkness is winning, remember those three hours of supernatural darkness while Jesus hung on the cross.

All hope seemed gone. Then the sun began to shine again. The supernatural Light of the world, God's only begotten Son, overcame the darkness. Jesus rose as the light of the world Who is victorious over Satan, sin, and the grave.

King David encouraged himself in the Lord. You can do the same. The Word always triumphs. His resurrection power continues to work in us (Ephesians 3: 20) even when we don't feel like it. And I believe it's perfectly biblical to ask the Lord to send His angels to strengthen us, just as they did for Him in Luke 22:43.

A Prayer for Encouragement:

Lord Jesus, it gets discouraging at times when it seems the darkness is winning. I am tempted to doubt, like Thomas, unless I also can see and touch. You were gracious enough to manifest Your resurrected body to Thomas, even though he doubted. Lord I want the blessing of believing even what I do not yet see. But sometimes I need to see and touch. Sometimes I need the encouragement of seeing improvement in the natural. I know You hear my prayer, O Lord. I rejoice because the answer is on the way, no matter how deep the darkness. Amen.

†

Foolishness To The Natural Mind

The first time I saw people falling down "under the power" and lying there in a trance-like state, I said to the Lord, You have to show me this in the Bible before I can accept it. He did. When God does things that are out of our ordinary experience, we tend to try explain it by what we know as natural. I have learned over the years that I Cor. 2: 14 is so very true.

"The natural man does not receive the things of the spirit of God, because they are foolishness to him." There are 33 Bible verses about falling before the Lord. Some of them are voluntary and some are not. Here's one example."Jesus therefore, knowing all things that should come upon him, went forth, and said to the officers, who are you looking for? They answered, Jesus of Nazareth. Jesus said to them, I am he.... As soon as he said, *I am he*, they went backward, and fell to the ground," (John 18:4-).I have included commentary by Biblical scholar, author and teacher Rick Renner: "Just as the Roman soldiers and temple police were preparing to arrest Jesus, a supernatural power was suddenly released that was so strong, it literally knocked an entire band of 300 to 600 soldiers backward. In fact, the verse says they went backward and fell to the ground. The words 'to the ground' are taken from the Greek word *chamai*, which depicts these soldiers falling abruptly and hitting the ground *hard*.

The power unexpectedly, suddenly, and forcefully knocked these troops and temple police flat."What a shock it must have been for those military men! The mere words of Jesus were enough to overwhelm and overpower them.

After Jesus proved He couldn't be taken by force, He willfully surrendered to them, knowing that it was all a part of the Father's plan for the redemption of mankind. But it's important to understand that *no one took Him*. It was Jesus' *voluntary choice* to go with the troops."The Jesus we serve is powerful! There is no force strong enough to resist His power. No sickness, financial turmoil, relational problems, political force — *absolutely nothing* has enough power to resist the supernatural power of Jesus Christ!

When the Great **I AM** opens His mouth and speaks, every power that attempts to defy Him or His Word is pushed backward and shaken until it staggers, stumbles, and falls to the ground!" **There is nothing more powerful than the Word of the Lord.**

Write Isa. 55: 11 here.

†

Recipe For Divine Health

There are many dietary laws in Deuteronomy concerning the eating of various kinds of "clean" meat. The Passover lamb had to be eaten at a single setting. I will add this. When you stop to think about it, *death is God's enemy* (I Cor. 15: 26).

I have come to believe that it was never God's perfect will for animals to die in order that people might eat (Isa. 65: 25). God has a perfect will, an acceptable will, and a permissive will (Rom. 12: 2). He allowed man to eat the flesh of animals after Noah's flood. That was His permissive will. But His perfect will was that man eat every plant bearing seed and green herbs as stated in Genesis 1: 29. Consider also that man lived up to 900 years and more until after the flood when meat was added to the diet.

Over the centuries, the Jews who practiced the dietary laws given to Moses, have been healthier and far less susceptible to the common chronic diseases that so many experience on an animal-based diet. Knowing that what people eat is so important to them that the Hebrews were ready to turn back to slavery in Egypt just so they could enjoy garlic and leeks, it is often difficult to persuade someone that the quality of life can be greatly improved by eating God's original plant-based diet. However, I am experiencing health benefits in my own body that certainly make it worthwhile.

When I was diagnosed with cancer in 1993, the Lord spoke to my heart: feed your immune system and starve the disease. Feed your faith and starve your doubts. That, my friend, is the recipe to divine health.

Example prayer:

Father, I see that all food is to be consecrated as we ask Your blessing upon it. I also see that there are very real benefits from eating the foods which You created for the body so that it functions as You intend. Give me wisdom to choose what is best. Thank You Lord. Amen.

†

Are Your Children Prey? Not If You Can Help it! (And You Can!)

The spies frightened the Hebrews into fear of giants and convinced them they could not possess the land. God's promise had gone forth that they would possess the land, but instead they chose to believe a lie. Who is it that always dares to question the Word of God and rob us of His promises?

Look what happened to their children. "But your little ones, which ye have said should be a prey (for the enemy) I will bring in and they shall know the land which you have despised," (Num. 14: 28-31).

Words are so very important. We want our children to enter into the blessings of God (Acts 2: 39). What do we say when we see them struggling? Making poor choices? Running with the wrong crowd? We speak faith, not fear. We speak the covenant blessings over them daily. We do not agree with doubt and fear of dangerous giants which threaten to destroy them. We do not **say** they are "prey" for the enemy.

Example prayer for children:

Father, I come to the throne of grace to put You in remembrance of Your word. I declare my children are not falling prey to the enemy. You said You will contend with him that contends with me and You

will save my children (Isa. 49: 25). I put You in remembrance of Your words. You said my children are blessed according to Psalm 103: 17. They receive the promise of the Holy Spirit, (Acts 2: 39). By the authority of Jesus' name, I cancel the assignment of the enemy against them. According to 2 Cor. 10: 5, I take authority over every stronghold the enemy has planted in their minds—abuse, rejection, false teaching, anger, fear, pride—and cast it down by the blood of the Lamb. I loose the power of Your word to replace all thoughts that exalt themselves against the knowledge of God. I say Your angels watch over them (Psa. 34: 7). I speak the blood of the Lamb over them and ask the Holy Spirit to guide them into all truth. They shall "know the promised land." Praise be to the Lord. Amen.

†

No Longer Natural People

Bible readers know that "Satan, the ruler of this world, will be cast out" (John 16: 11). However, this doesn't happen until the second coming. In John 17, Jesus says He is going away. Then He asks the Father *not to take His followers out of the world* but to protect them from the evil one.

Obviously, we need divine protection from the enemy who is compared to a roaring lion walking through the earth seeking whom he may devour (I Pet. 5:8).

Jesus promised, "You shall receive power after the Holy Spirit comes upon you," (Luke 10: 19; John 14; Acts chapter One).

"Power" in the New Testament Greek Lexicon is "Dunamis." It means: "miraculous power, ability" (Strong's); "capability, ability to perform miracles; not merely power capable of action, but, power in action."

Supernatural power is not merely for resisting a second helping of ice cream. Dunamis is power to heal, set the captive free, heal the sick, raise the dead, cast out devils. I didn't say that. God did (Matt. 10: 8; Mark 16: 17-18).

God wants His people empowered to bless others, just as He modeled for us in His earthly walk. When believers are filled with the Holy Spirit, they are no longer merely natural people. They have access to the supernatural realm. That's you and me. **Faith says what God says.**

Write Matt. 10: 8 here and speak it over your own life.

Example prayer:

Father, I am not satisfied to do what I can achieve merely by my own human strength, for then You do not get the glory. I invite You to work Your mighty works through the weakness of my human flesh in order to bless others. Amen.

†

Can You Say All Is Well When In Bitter Distress?

One of my favorite Bible characters doesn't even have a name. She is the Shunamite woman, a woman of great faith, described in II Kings 4: 8-37. She is the mother of a miracle baby boy, *spoken* into her life by the prophet Elisha. When the child suffered a fatal heat stroke one day, she did not acknowledge that fact. Instead, three times that same day, this woman declared, "All is well."

How many know that facts are subject to change? She had the opportunity to tell her husband their son was dead. But she did not. Instead, she said, "All is well." Twice more, she encountered people and said "All is well." If she had answered, "My son is dead," most likely she would have begun to weep and wail. That would have been a natural reaction.

The Shunamite mother certainly was not without natural emotion. Elisha saw her coming and knew she was in "bitter distress." She fell at his feet and refused to let go of him. He followed her back to the upper room, which had been constructed for his occasional overnight stays. There Elisha prayed over the boy until he sat up and was restored to his mother. She spoke her faith, *all is well*, instead of her bitter distress, and she received her son back from the dead.

Example prayer:

Father, I won't let go of your Word, which promises life. Even though it looks like the thing I have asked for is dead or dying. All things are possible to them who believe, and I am a believer. Thank you for strength to stand when I feel bitter distress. I look to You and I can say, all is well. Amen.

†

No Root Equals No Fruit

We have talked about the parable of sower. The Lord impressed on my heart how the parable of the sower is foundational. Jesus said if we don't understand it, how can we understand how the kingdom works. (Mark 4: 13). So, I don't hesitate to mention the layers of truth in this parable again.

I know the seed is the word. If I don't have the word rooted and grounded deeply in the good soil of my heart, I cannot bear fruit.

Then I saw it! I must be able to say, "It is written . . ." in order to resist the fowls of the air who come to steal the seed. I can speak the victory verses when the enemy tells me I'm defeated.

I cannot simply memorize a scripture and repeat it every once in a while. It has to take root. Deep root. Deuteronomy 22:9–11 reads, "Do not plant two kinds of seed in your vineyard; if you do, not only the crops you plant but also the fruit of the vineyard will be defiled.

What does that mean Lord?

Oh, I see it! The enemy sows his seeds of doubt. He lies, gets us to question the Word, "Has God said?" and steals the seeds that are not deeply rooted.

Words of doubt can steal the seed and destroy the harvest. Doubt words become an evil root of unbelief.

But Lord, Your word is incorruptible seed. That's

right. It is unchanging, settled forever in heaven, and I watch over My word to perform it. Get it deeply rooted, nourished, pull the weeds, and the harvest will come.

And the more seed you plant, the greater the harvest! Write 2 Cor. 9: 6.

Example prayer:

Father, in Jesus' name, I make a demand on the good seed of faith in my heart to rise up and drive out any doubt that tries to lie to me and make me focus on what is seen in the natural instead of what is *not yet* seen in the supernatural. Amen.

†

What If The Worst Happens?

We all want to avoid the worst and expect God to deliver us from evil.

But what if the worst happens? God is still there. What if a loved one dies? God heals both in natural time and in eternity. Without being healed eternally, being healed in natural time is meaningless. However, a believer who leaves this world in a sick body has the promise of eternal wellness with the Lord. Even through grief, we can rejoice and look for a glad reunion. We sorrow not as the world sorrows (I Thess. 4: 13).

God never promised there would be no tears. He promised to wipe them away. He never promised I would not go through the valley of the shadow death. He promised He would be there with me and comfort me. Disappointment can cause a person to become angry with God—to decide that God is somehow to blame for not preventing a tragedy or answering our prayers the way we expected. Doctor Dave Walker, Physician and author of the popular book, *God in the ICU*, says, "Our faith should always be in the goodness of God and not in the expected outcome of things we are hoping for." He also observes that, impressive as the testimonies of healing miracles are, there is nothing more profound than a victorious attitude in those who are living with difficulty. He names heroes of the faith who live with missing limbs, terrible scars, etc., fearless witnesses for Jesus. Dave Roever, Joni Erickson Tada and soul-surfer Bethany Hamilton come to mind. **Write Job 42: 12 and Rom. 8: 28.**

†

Do We Expect Too Much From God Or Not Enough?

I must admit I'm like Moses. If I see a snake, I run the other way.

The Lord never promised Paul he wouldn't suffer a snake bite. However, He promised authority over serpents and scorpions and over all the power of the enemy. Remember how Moses' serpent swallowed up the magicians' snakes? That's victory.

God never promised Paul that his storm-tossed ship would not sink. Instead He promised the lives of all on board would be spared. The ship was lost, but not a single life.

The Lord never promised Paul he wouldn't be stoned. In fact, He promised Paul *would* suffer tribulation for his apostleship. Fear of persecution did not stop Paul from obeying his calling, and the Lord raised him up from what was certainly death by stoning, and Paul walked to Derbe the next day.

When the deadly viper fastened on Paul while he was building a fire, the observers soon gave God all the glory because they realized he should have died. No matter what the enemy did to try to stop Paul in his tracks, it resulted in more people being saved and more glory to the Lord.

No matter what the enemy brings against a believer, God is able to turn it around for good. Even if the loss seems irreparable.

Example prayer:

Father, I thank You that I can trust in Your word, no matter what snake 'bites' come against me. I get weary at times, but You said let the weak say I am strong. So, I say I am strong in the Lord. I can do all things through Christ Who strengthens me. I declare the end—victory—from the beginning. In Your power and might, my enemies shall not triumph over me. Amen.

†

Three kinds Of faith

Mentioned in the Bible are at least three kinds of faith, apart from great faith and little faith.

A measure of faith: There is a measure of faith given to every man (Ro. 12: 3). This is the faith which enables a person to call on the name of the Lord and be saved. It is the kind of faith which God gifts to everyone in Eccl. 3: 11. Growing faith: When the disciples asked Jesus to increase their faith, He answered, "Faith comes by hearing and hearing by the word of God," Romans 10: 17. This is faith that a believer _increases_ when he studies, reads, repeats, and meditates on the Word. This faith separates the diligent seekers, who are promised a reward, from the average passive believer who leaves it all up to God to do whatever.

A supernatural gift of faith: This comes through the operation of the Holy Spirit, (1 Cor. 12: 9). It is a supernatural faith that enables a believer to perform signs and wonders. It cannot be developed, earned, or exercised apart from the Holy Spirit. The gift of this kind of faith is usually for performing the miraculous, and it is always to glorify the Father.

Not all have the gift of faith mentioned in I Cor. Chapter 12. That is a gift bestowed through the operation of the Holy Spirit. Believers are instructed to be most concerned with the second faith mentioned above, the growing and developing kind of faith to move mountains. It can only happen by giving attention to God's word. This faith will move a person into the supernatural realm by studying to show himself approved unto God, a workman that does not need to feel ashamed, (2 Tim. 2: 14).

I firmly believe that when Jesus said signs will follow them that believe, He intends for every believer to heal the sick, cast out demons, speak with new tongues, raise the dead. Most of us do not get to experience this. Why is that? Is the Lord waiting on His body to rise up, exercise the authority He gave us, and boldly obey His command? The Lord Spoke to My Heart

How highly do you esteem the Word of God?

God spoke through the prophet Hosea to say: "My people perish through ignorance of My Word," (Hosea 4: 6). Ignorance is a dangerous thing.

If ignoring God's Word can be fatal, then esteeming His Word can lead to life (John 6: 63).

People use the Name of Jesus in all kinds of disrespectful and blasphemous ways. The poison of vipers is on their lips (Psalm 140: 3). However, there is no other name under heaven whereby men may be saved.

The way of escape from every trial, temptation, fear, and affliction is provided in and through the Word (I Cor. 10: 13).

How highly do I esteem the Word of God? It is my meditation every morning. That's when the Lord speaks to me most often. That's when He says, "Be still and know that I am God."Throughout the day I long to hear His voice. A fool has said in his heart, there is no god.

An even greater fool knows there's a God and fails to seek Him. **Faith says what God says.**

Write Heb. 2: 3.

The Identity Crisis

"I just need to find out who I am." This was a common phrase in the 70's and even still today. The words, "I AM," are the key.

You will never know who you really are until you meet Him who is the great I Am. He gave Adam and Eve their true identity. They reflected His image.

The serpent tempted them to question their identity, to think they could become "like gods, knowing good and evil" (Gen. 3: 5). The identity they got was one of guilt and shame.

Simon the disciple answered the eternal question, "Who do you say that I am?" He answered without question, "You are Christ, the Son of God." Immediately, Jesus gave Peter a new identity. "You are Peter. Flesh and blood did not reveal this to you but My Father in Heaven (that's supernatural revelation knowledge) and on this rock I shall build my church (Matt. 16: 17).

Some believe Peter is the rock. Others believe supernatural revelation is the Rock and the keys to the kingdom. Certainly no one comes to the Father without supernatural revelation of Who Christ is (Matt. 28: 18). But *what if* Jesus was pointing to Himself as the Rock?

Jesus is described as the Rock of salvation in Psalm 78: 35 and 58 more Bible verses. Significantly, Jesus describes Himself as the chief corner*stone* (not Peter) in whom the whole building (church or body of believers) is joined together and the gates of hell shall not prevail against it.

Without Jesus, we have no advocate, no mediator to defend us against Satan (I Tim. 2: 5). Without Jesus, the rock of our salvation, there is no way to prevail against the gates of hell. Every believer who receives Jesus as Redeemer, Messiah, the only way, truth, and life, becomes spiritually born into the invisible kingdom of God, becomes a new creation, and has a new identity (2 Cor. 5:17).

God looks at us, not as sinners, but as the very righteousness of God in Christ (2 Cor. 5; 21)—not because of anything we did or did not do, but because of what He did on the cross. Every temptation the liar brings against us is based on questioning that identity. He lost his identity as Lucifer, the worship leader in heaven, and became Satan, the evil one. That's what he's been trying to label every person since his fall.

†

Why The Shepherds?

Have you ever wondered why the Father announced the birth of His Son to a group of shepherds? Jesus was born in Bethlehem. Scholars believe it was at Migdal Edar, significantly the birthing place of the **sacrificial lambs** to be offered in the Temple. This hamlet is named in Micah, 4:8 as the "tower of the flock." Migdal Edar was very near the temple in Bethlehem.

The shepherds were specifically trained for this royal, priestly task. They were to verify that the lambs were without blemish, no bones having been broken during birth or thereafter, and without any defect. They also swaddled the newborn lambs in white linen. The angels announced Christ's birth to these specially-trained shepherds.

Perhaps unknowingly, these shepherds were witnesses performing their priestly duty that the babe was without blemish. They beheld the true sacrificial "Lamb of God, which taketh away the sin of the world," John 1: 29 (KJV).

He was wrapped in white swaddling clothes, just like the newborn sacrificial lambs. He was placed in a manger, a feeding trough. Jesus said of Himself that He is the true bread come down from Heaven and when we feed our spirits on this living spiritual bread (His Word in John 6: 63) we have life.

Kings later bowed to Him, signifying that He is the

King of Kings. All circumstances of His birth were fulfillments of specific prophecies, which is how God confirms to the world that His word is true (Josh 23: 24).

Father, I'm so thankful the perfect Lamb's sacrifice cancels my debt of sin. I am able to partake of the true bread of Heaven, instead of temporary manna. I'm so thankful I have life in my spirit, soul, and body (Prov. 4: 22). Amen.

†

Give No Place To The Devil

Give no place to the devil (Eph. 4: 27). How do we accomplish that? What does it mean to give place to the devil? Strife is one sure way. We are warned never to let the sun go down on our wrath, "so that your prayers may not be hindered," (I Pet. 3: 7). An awesome thought.

Anger can hinder our prayers. There are also plenty of scriptures about negative people who should be avoided, however, when something bad happens to an enemy we are warned: "Do not gloat when your enemy falls; when they stumble, do not let your heart rejoice, (Prv. 24: 17) or the Lord will see and disapprove and turn His wrath away from him." Job 31: 29 "If I have rejoiced at my enemy's misfortune or gloated over the trouble that came to him—I have not allowed my mouth to sin . . . "

Bitter words do damage. "Your own soul is nourished when you speak kindly. *You destroy yourself when you are cruel.*" (Prov. 11: 17). In other words, we reap what we sow. Cruel words come back to us because they give place to the devil. The atmosphere is changed. The Spirit of peace, love, and joy is grieved, (Eph. 4: 30) and will remove His presence.

This does not mean that we excuse every wrong or evil doing. It does mean that we overcome evil with good: "If your enemy is hungry, feed him; if he is thirsty, give him something to drink. In doing this, you will heap burning coals on his head."

Do not be overcome by evil, but overcome evil with good. Romans 12:19-21 That takes wisdom, good judgment, patience, and the Holy Spirit's help, because our natural fleshly self wants to gloat when someone who has behaved wickedly falls into troubles.

†

An Unanswered Prayer?

I asked the Lord once if He ever had a prayer that went unanswered. He immediately took me to the gospel of Matthew 6: 9, where He taught the disciples about prayer.

Suddenly it became apparent to me. When Jesus said, "Your kingdom come," He was not pleading with the Father for this to happen. The Lord was issuing a *decree* for the kingdom, which is "not of this world," to be established here "on earth as it is in heaven." (Job 22: 28). He did not have to beg for it, since He knew already that this is the Father's will. He was speaking like His Heavenly Father speaks—declaring the end from the beginning (Isa. 46: 10).

What an amazing thought. Those words, *spoken* by believers in agreement with the Lord Jesus Christ for centuries, have the power to usher in the kingdom of God on earth as it is in heaven (Matt. 18: 18). The Father's will is for no more tears, sickness, death, or troubles here on earth as it is in heaven. What a powerful decree.

That prayer has not yet been answered. Satan is still the god of this world. The unseen kingdom of Light is here now, visible only in the spirits and works of born-again believers (Matt. 5: 16).

However, that prayer is soon to be answered at the return of the Lord. That's cause for rejoicing!

Faith Says What God Says by Harriett Ford

Father, I pray these words of Jesus. Let Your will be done and Your kingdom come on earth as it is in Heaven. Thine is the kingdom, the power, and the glory forever and ever. Come Lord Jesus! Amen.

†

Looking At Natural Circumstances Instead Of The Supernatural?

We all do that most of the time. In the Numbers 13: 25-33 account, the ten spies compared themselves to the giants in the land instead of comparing the giants to God. Whatever giants you may be facing today, they are only greater if you allow them to be.

Greater is He that is in you (the Holy Spirit) than he that is in the world (Satan, the god of this world). All you need to do is speak God's promise, "we are well able to defeat the giants," like Joshua and Caleb did.

God does not go back on His word. He honored their faith. Of all Israel's fighting men, only Joshua and Caleb got to enter the promised land and they were well able (still strong in their 80's) to defeat the giants.

Looking only at the natural circumstances is focusing on the giants. Looking at God is focusing on His word. No weapon formed against you shall prosper.

Father, I choose to believe Your report and no report in the natural realm that contradicts what Your word says. True wisdom has two sides, both natural and supernatural.

I will act with wisdom in the natural realm, and I will act by faith in the supernatural realm, no matter how foolish I may appear. I choose to renew my mind according to what You have promised. I

am well able to defeat the giants which try to prevent me from entering into the fullness of Your promises to me. Amen.

†

How Can Both Be True?

An auto-antonym is a word with multiple meanings of which one is the reverse of another. For example, the word cleave can mean "to cut apart" or "to bind together." Some difficult doctrines in the Bible may be viewed in that category.

The unsearchable riches of the incomparable wisdom of God are described in the Apostle Paul's words, "His ways are past finding out."How can two apparent contradictions both be true? And yet they simply are. God has two first born sons. He names Israel His "firstborn son" called out of Egypt in Ex. 4: 22. In the New Testament it's Jesus. "For those whom he foreknew he also predestined to be conformed to the image of his Son, in order that he might be the firstborn among many brothers. (Romans 8:29).

Jesus, one hundred percent man and one hundred percent God. (He laid aside His divinity (Phil. 2: 7) and operated as a man with the same body of flesh as Adam's (I Cor. 15: 45-49). He was able to perform miracles under the anointing of the Holy Spirit which He sent to all believers. Good news!You must lose your life in order to save it. You must give in order to receive.

When you are weak, then you are strong. You are chosen by God, but you also must choose Him. You must be blind in order to see best in the supernatural kingdom (walking by faith and not by sight). His ways are past finding out, but we are told to seek Him.

Jesus is the Lion of Judah. He is also the Lamb of God. What could be more opposite? Whoever would be great among you must be a servant. We must grow and mature in our faith and yet become as little children. Our sins are forgiven past, present and future, but continuing a life of sin can cause spiritual death (Matt. 7:21-23).

The grace of God has appeared to every man (Titus 2: 11), yet we know that few will find the path to life. His ways are past finding out. Yet we are told to seek Him get understanding and wisdom. There are names which were NOT written in the Book of Life from before the foundation of the world, (Rev. 17: 8) and yet Peter says it is NOT God's will that any should perish and that all would come to repentance. How can this be? How can both be true at the same time? If we could explain it and have perfect understanding, we wouldn't be living by faith. We simply trust in the goodness, the faithfulness and the mercy of our all mighty God.

TESTIMONIES

Whom the Son sets free is free indeed. There are hundreds of thousands of testimonies from people who are learning how prayers of authority are setting people free from every manner of disease. I am including only one. The following shows clearly the steps of faith in action.

Hannah Terradez

Carlie Terradez's testimony is a perfect example of how the woman with the issue of blood received her healing. Her Faith, Her Words, And her Action.

I'm going to talk about one of my favorite modern-day miracles. We're going to look at six things this couple did to activate their child's miracle.

Little Hannah Terradez suffered for three agonizing years with a severe digestive disorder that kept her from processing food. Medical science had done everything they knew to do. She survived only with a feeding tube. Doctors sent her home to die. However, her parents, Ashley and Carlie, knew Jesus as healer. Carlie had been miraculously healed of epilepsy, which she had suffered from childhood. After three years of begging God for Hannah's life with no improvement, the couple heard from well-meaning ministers and other people that they should "let her go." Hannah had been through enough. It must not be God's will to heal her.

But like the woman with the issue of blood, they intended to press through. First, they <u>heard</u> the Word that Jesus is not only Savior but healer (Acts 10: 38) and that healing is His will (Matt. 8:3). They continued to hear this message and to renew their natural thinking to supernatural truth. Faith comes by hearing the Word, *and hearing (*Rom. 10: 17). They listened to Andrew Wommack's message of the healing gospel over and over. Second, they spoke their faith in <u>agreement</u>.

Like the woman with the issue of blood in Mark Chapter five who said in her heart that if she could just touch the hem of His garment, she knew she would be healed, Ashley and Carlie decided to take Hannah to Walsall, England where Andrew had come for a healing conference.

As the family packed into the car, Ashley turned to his wife and said, "Carlie, we have never heard any teacher who is so positive, that it is *always* God's will to heal. Everyone else *tells us sometimes God does not heal*. Andrew rejects this, and now, so do I. When Andrew prays for Hannah, I believe she will be healed." (Luke 17: 6; Mark 11: 23-24)."I agree 100 percent," Carlie replied. (Matt. 18: 19). When two agree together as touching anything it shall be done.Third, they believed that they received her healing by faith with *no outward evidence.* At the end of the long day, when the crying and suffering child had finally fallen into an exhausted sleep, Andrew prayed a simple prayer over her. Amazingly and by faith alone, Ashley and Carlie believed that their daughter received her healing. Faith is the evidence of things that are not seen (Heb. 11: 1).

Hannah continued to sleep for another thirty minutes. This gave Ashley and Carlie time to discuss what they should do to "walk out" the healing they believed she had just received. Together they discussed the kinds of mild foods Hannah might eat to ease her body back toward a normal diet. After such severe deprivation, a sudden intake of the wrong kind of food could kill her. They wanted to act in faith, but they also wanted to be wise. Can you imagine the what-ifs going through their minds?

Fourth, they testified. Let the redeemed of the Lord say so. When Hannah awoke, she was completely calm. Ashley bent over her and said, "Hannah, while you were asleep, Jesus healed you. "Without hesitation, she brightened and said, "I want to eat. I want to go to McDonald's!" Carlie looked at Ashley dumbfounded. "She's always been ahead of us in faith," she said. Hannah's five-year-old brother Zachary piped up, "Now that Hannah's healed, she won't need her tube anymore." To that, Hannah added, "Yeah, and I can eat anything I want now!"

Little Hannah was declaring her faith. Fifth, the parents *acted* on faith that she was healed. Faith without works is dead (James 2:17). That settled it. Carlie promptly unplugged Hannah's feeding tube. She took the bag of costly medicines that had been used hour-by-hour to sustain her life and hid them away. She did not allow fear to dictate what to do next, although the what-ifs were no doubt screaming at her imagination.

As Ashley watched his daughter eat, he could hardly contain his excitement. He sent a text message to his mother, Linda, in Essex, England: "Praise God. Hannah was healed! She has been eating like a trooper! Jesus has healed her 100 percent. Just like the Word tells us so in First Peter 2:24."

After the meal, the Terradez family got back in the car to return to the final evening session of the conference. They were bouncing with excitement and divine energy. They would testify before the group that it is always God's will to heal, and all we have to do is believe and take our authority in Christ. But suddenly, a terrible sound sent a shiver of fear through everyone in the car. From her safety chair in the rear seat, Hannah began to gag and cough. This familiar sound was an absolute precursor, always leading to vomiting, violent pain, and diarrhea! Her brothers began to duck for cover. Sixth, they had to exercise authority over the illness. Hearing the familiar gagging sound, Ashley remembered Andrew's teaching about *not speaking to God about a problem but speaking to the problem about God.* (Luke 10: 18-19; Mark 11: 23-24). He turned in his seat and spoke to the familiar symptoms, "Choking, gagging, in the name of Jesus, I command you to stop!"

That is what a prayer of faith based on the authority of the Law of the Spirit of Life sounds like. No begging prayers like before and like Moses prayed for Miriam in Numbers 12: 13 (which was based on the Law of sin). Even little 3-yr.-old Hannah did not beg. She had been saying, "Thank You Jesus for healing me," in her prayers long before her healing manifested.

A calm settled over Hannah. She swallowed and stopped choking. The boys emerged from hiding. In another moment, she was laughing and playing with her brothers again. In the days ahead, this scene was repeated once more with the same result. The parents resisted the devil (James 4: 7; Luke 10: 18-19; Mark 4:4).If Ashley had not known what to do when symptoms returned, the fowls of the air would surely have robbed Hannah of her healing (Luke 8: 12-13). Her parents would have been saying, "I guess she wasn't healed after all." They would have been walking by natural sight, instead of SON light. From that day in Walsall, England when Carlie disconnected the feeding tube, Hannah has never used it again. Nor have her parents used any of the expensive medicines that had once been so necessary for Hannah's survival. Carlie Terradez now ministers healing at Andrew Wommack's Charis Bible College in Colorado. Her daughter Hannah is an adult, married and happily serving the Lord Who healed her. Faith says what God says. Carlie boldly proclaims that healing is always God's will. Rev. 12: 11 - We overcome by the blood of the Lamb and the word of our testimony. What is the word of our testimony? We have victory in Christ Jesus. Amen!

The story of little Hannah Terradez can be found at http://www.awmi.net/video/healing/hannah/ the site for Andrew Wommack's Healing testimonies.

Afterword

Why Isn't Everyone Healed?

Fellow Believer seeking answers to this never-ending mystery . . .why did Sister Faithful die when so many prayers went up for her?

This question assumes that Jesus should heal only the deserving faithful and the righteous few. Actually, He healed sinners, prostitutes, lepers, even a soldier who came to arrest Him.

Now we see through a glass darkly. I don't pretend to know all the answers; however, the four most common scriptural reasons are: Unbelief, the traditions of men which make the word of none effect, hardness of heart, ignorance of the word, and unforgiveness. Faith, which works by love, will not activate healing in an unforgiving heart. All these blockers to healing can be easily overcome by spending time in the Word, renewing the mind, and more importantly asking the Holy Spirit for revelation knowledge of these truths.

Some people believe that it is somehow a lack of reverence for God when a sick person continues to persevere in seeking supernatural healing in the hope of living a full life span. That train of thought assumes that God's will is for the sick to stay sick. And I do not deny that many devout people do. There are reasons. God has secrets and mysteries. And yes, sin has consequences.

Believers have the opportunity to repent, to choose to live under the law of the Spirit of Life in Christ Jesus, and to walk in the supernatural realm, the Son Light of Genesis 1: 11.

No matter the argument, divine healing is a confirmation of Christ's deity, according to Jesus Himself. In John 14:11, Jesus said to believe Him because of the *works* He did. When His cousin John the Baptist apparently began to doubt if Jesus really was the Messiah (Luke 7:20-22) Jesus replied: "Go back and report to John what you hear and see: the blind receive sight, the lame walk, those who have leprosy are cured, the deaf hear, the dead are raised, and the good news is preached to the poor. Blessed is the man who does not fall away on account of me." In other words, *believe because of these works*. He is the same, yesterday, today, and forever.

Readers who have read this entire book know that a prayer of doubt doesn't heal anyone. I will add that even when the prayer of faith is spoken and there is no healing manifested, that does not mean healing isn't God's perfect will.

A look at 2 Peter 3: 8-10 clearly shows it is not God's will for any to perish, but for all to come to repentance. The same can be said about God's will for healing, which is why our daughter does not have asthma, scoliosis, or a heart murmur today. Thanks be to God who healed her.

Not everyone receives salvation. Not everyone receives healing, but that doesn't mean it isn't God's will. He made the provision for both. It's up to us to receive.

I can also recommend many ministers whose healing ministries are successful—not a hundred percent, but then what evangelist has a hundred percent of salvations at every meeting? I debated whether to name them, because so many people have tuned them out and many have greatly discredited their ministries.

I, myself, turned my back on the faith teachings for a few years, thinking *I tried what they said and it didn't work.* However, as I continued diligently to seek truth, the Holy Spirit led me through the Word on the subject of healing, and without even realizing it, I came full circle right back to the fundamental teachings of such men of faith as: Kenneth Hagin, Charles Capps, Jerry Savelle, David Ingles, Ken and Gloria Copeland, Andrew Wommack, Robert Morris, Billy Burke, Marilyn Hickey, Dr. Sandra Kennedy, John G. Lake, Dr. Lilian B. Yoemans, Smith Wigglesworth, and many more. Satan despises these men and women of faith and continues to persecute and discredit them. Thanks be to God, He uses imperfect people who mess up and make mistakes, but who also keep on doing what He has called them to do in the face of persecution. **GOD IS STILL A MIRACLE WORKER**.

Have faith in God because with God *all things* are possible. Who wants to argue with that? The thief who comes to steal the good seed of faith, of course. I determined long ago, this subject is too important to neglect. While I am not always successful at praying the prayer of faith for others, I am still seeing success. Anyone who studies to show himself approved, who continues to seek, knock, and ask has a promise from the Lord. That one will find answers.

Let all who seek Him rejoice and be glad! You are appointed to victory, not defeat. Amen.

The End

Copyright ©
H.L Ford 2019

The author retains all rights,
including the right to reproduce
this book, including all text,
art and illustrations, in any form.

ISBN: 9781793369550

Third Edition
Designed and Formatted by
Meredith House Publishing

Made in the USA
Monee, IL
01 February 2021